D1404036

"Lisa McLeod is a voice we need."

—**Liz Kahn**, Managing Editor, *The Buffalo News*

"Lisa McLeod is the only writer I know who can talk about sex and cereal in the same sentence and make you laugh so hard the Muslix comes snorting out of your nose."

—**Michael Alvear**, HBO host and syndicated columnist

"*Finding Grace* reminds those on a spiritual path that taking one-self too seriously can be an obstacle to bliss."

—**David Simon**, MD, Deepak Chopra Center for Wellbeing

"It's fantastic. Lisa serves up insights about work, marriage, friend-ship, and parenting in such funny ways you don't even realize you're learning something."

—**Cynthia Good**, Editor-in-Chief, *PINK* magazine

"Don't let Lisa's humor fool you; she'll have you laughing, and sud-denly your life will change."

—**Heather Gemmen**, columnist and bestselling author of *Startling Beauty*

Finding Grace

Finding Grace

When You Can't Even Find
Clean Underwear

Lisa Earle McLeod

The Meaning of Life and
Why Other People are
So *#$%@! Annoying

jefferson press

ISBN 978-0-977808-63-2
Library of Congress Catalog Card Number: 2006939898

Editing by Henry Oehmig
Cover Illustration by Joan Perrin-Falquet
Book Design by Fiona Raven

First Printing April 2007
Printed in Canada

Published by Jefferson Press

jefferson press

P.O. Box 115
Lookout Mountain, TN 37350

For

Bob McLeod,
the other half of my heart,

and

Lisa Daily,
the other half of my brain.

Contents

Prologue

People often ask me how I can write about fast food, fake boobs, reality TV, and annoying in-laws and still consider it a spiritual experience.

I guess it's because I think most of our problems are really people problems and that people problems are actually spiritual problems in disguise. And if I can help us laugh at the lunacy of our lives, I'm doing my part to help the universe become sane.

I call this book *Finding Grace* because I believe that's what we all secretly crave; a graceful, peaceful existence that transcends demanding bosses, corrupt politicians, and imperfect spouses.

Webster's Dictionary defines *grace* as "a divinely given talent or blessing." I do believe that we humans have been blessed. We're blessed by the beauty of the other souls who surround us each day. Unfortunately, most of those lovely, little souls are trapped inside hugely annoying personalities that bug the living heck out of us.

But if I could reach into the heart of humanity and impart one message, it's this: You don't have to control the chaos to find the peace within.

You don't have to be organized; you don't have to be skinny; you don't have to make gobs of cash; and you don't even have to have an enlightened spouse or family to be happy.

I fancy myself as a faux intellectual and a spiritual seeker. Although I read and enjoy many of those "find your inner bliss" books, I often suspect that the people who write them don't have fifty-seven emails, three screaming kids, and six piles of dirty laundry competing for their attention while they meditate.

I'm also a person of great faith, both in God and the future of the human condition, but there's nothing I enjoy more than poking fun at some of the hypocrisy found in organized religion.

And so that's the crux of this book. It's about the dullards and the divine. I want to show you how you can live in an irrational, infuriating, inconvenient world and still find the grace to enjoy it.

We humans have created a nuthouse of global proportions. Yet despite our Botox-injecting, email-addicted, money-grubbing, marriage-wrecking ways, in our hearts, we are truly amazing. We are both flawed and fabulous at the same time. And watching humanity in action is the best reality show in town.

I wish you peace, I wish you joy, and I wish you the grace to discover how wonderful you already are.

I

Why Are Other People So Fascinating & So Annoying?

*"The difference between stupidity and genius
is that genius has its limits."*

—ALBERT EINSTEIN

Nicotine Nirvana: Welcome to the Smoking State

Where have all the smokers gone?

They aren't allowed in restaurants, they've been barred from offices, and many hotels are now smoke-free. As best I can tell, half the smokers in America are trapped in a little glass room at the airport, defiantly puffing away while the rest of us scurry by, trying not to make eye contact.

I'm not a big fan of cigarettes, but I'm actually starting to feel sorry for all the smokers being publicly shunned. Spending your life huddled beside the dumpsters out back with only Joe Camel or the Marlboro Man to keep you company is no way to live.

Quitting is the obvious answer. But anybody who's ever watched a cancer patient hack up half a lung and then try to bum a drag from the oncology nurse knows it's not always that easy.

Instead of sentencing smokers to a life of stolen tokes in the parking lot, here's a better idea: Let's create an all-smoking state. It would be nicotine nirvana. All smoking, all the time.

Think about it. No more sneaking down to the loading dock to grab a cig before the big meeting. In the smoking state, it's just like the old days. Plunk your ashtray down in the middle of the table, and puff away while a blanket of smoke hangs over the room. No more huddling outside in the rain because your finicky in-laws are allergic. In the smoking state, the whole family lights up right at the kitchen table. Smoking churches would bring the faithful one step closer to heaven. Forget stealing a few quick drags in your car before the service begins. Pews would come equipped with butt cans and lighters. And the minister could keep one lit on the pulpit, gesturing with it during the sermon just like Dean Martin.

The big issue, of course, is deciding which state gets the "honor." At first I thought Virginia—after all, it's the original home of Big Tobacco. But then I realized there's a better solution: Louisiana. Picture it—we could solve two national problems at once: find a home for all the smokers and rebuild the Gulf Coast all in one fell swoop.

Imagine construction workers flocking to the Big Easy. What nicotine-addicted roofer wouldn't want work in the land of smoke and honey? Forget bothersome breaks. If workers could lay tile, roll carpet, and hang sheetrock with a cig dangling from their lower lips, rebuilding could be done in half the time. Steakhouses could ship their outlawed cigarette machines south. With nicotine dispensers on every corner, bayou residents could pick up a pack of smokes with the morning paper. The tax revenue alone would be astronomical.

Of course, there are a few challenges. For one thing, America's 47 million smokers won't all fit in Louisiana. So, if the idea really takes off, we may have to annex another state. There's also the tricky issue of healthcare. But this could be just the PR opportunity Big Tobacco's been waiting for. They could prove once and for all that smoking really is glamorous by picking up the healthcare costs for the entire state. However, with an entire state puffing away, there will undoubtedly be more deaths. Since much of Louisiana is below sea level, burials could be problematic. But mandatory cremation could ease the smokers' passage to the Big Ashtray in the sky.

Of course, there are children to consider. I feel sorry for smokers, but we can't subject kids to second-hand smoke. So residents would have to agree to a no-child policy. You pick up a birth control patch as you head into the state, and if you change your mind, you get your nicotine patch at the state line on the way out.

You know, now that I think about it, maybe this isn't such a good idea after all.

I mean, Louisiana already has enough problems without having to dispose of thirty-seven tons of cigarette butts. And if we couldn't figure out a way to get its people out of a hurricane, I doubt we'll be able to figure out how to administer a state-wide oxygen tank program either.

So unless another state wants to volunteer to go up in smoke, I guess Joe Camel and the Marlboro Man will have to stay trapped in the little glass hut at the airport forever.

The Six Friends Nobody Needs

Are you the friend everybody loves to hate?

We've all got a friend, or even friends, who just don't get it. No matter what the situation, they always turn it around, so it's about them. The common denominator in bad friend behavior is their self-absorption. But the symptoms manifest themselves differently depending on the folks involved.

I'm always in favor of giving people the benefit of the doubt, but here are six friends none of us need. You can cut them or cope, depending on the severity of their behavior.

1. THE WHINER. There's always a problem, and it's always happening to her. Nobody knows the troubles *she's* seen, but you better believe we're gonna hear about it. If your mother's dying in a hospital bed, but your friend's just had a fight with hers, guess who's going to monopolize the conversation?

Before you write her off, take a deep breath and remember whining is usually a bid for attention from somebody who doesn't know how to get it any other way. Next time she starts, tell her you'd rather hear about what's going right with her life. And if she doesn't have an answer, direct her to this great, new website: FindATherapist.com.

2. THE LEECH. He invites you over for "a few beers," and when you get there, you find yourself refinishing his deck. Or she asks you what you're doing tomorrow and when you say, "Nothing," she says, "Great, I need somebody to watch my kids." If they're not borrowing your best blouse or your power tools, they're asking you to feed their dog. They can't (or won't) handle their own lives, so they parcel off portions of it to everyone else.

The answer: Say "no" early and often. They'll either quit

asking so much, or they'll drop you, and you'll know they prefer having a servant over having a friend.

3. THE YAKKER. Thank God for caller ID. These people missed their calling as a carnival barker. Is she a friend or a walking monologue looking for a place to land? You could put down the phone for an hour, and she wouldn't miss a beat.

You can try giving her a muzzle (and if any of my pals are reading, for the record, I think I would look good in pink). But the most effective strategy is to imitate her behavior. Since Yakkers often assume that talking over people is a natural conversation style, they may actually be wondering why you've waited so long to jump in.

4. THE BUSY BEE. She's the PTA president, party organizer, and domestic diva—and you are nothing more than a mere blip on her overscheduled radar screen. You may think she's too busy for you, but the person she's really too busy for is herself.

Most overachievers got the message early on that they're the sum of their work, and nobody will like them if they slow down. You might want to remind these people what friendship really means. Imagine the look on their Type-A faces when you say, "I find your innermost thoughts fascinating, but your massive to-do list bores me to tears."

5. THE ADVISER. This one offers a steady stream of unsolicited feedback, just like the mother-in-law from hell. Whether they're trying to prove how smart they are or start their own counseling business, this friend has the answer for everything.

Lots of nodding and murmers of "I'll think about it," are an easy out. But if he or she is really getting under your skin, say, "I'm so glad I have you to tell me what to do. My life would be a mess if you weren't trying to run it." Smile while you're saying it, and they might not hit you.

6. THE BRAGGER. The message: Been there, done that, *and done it way better than you.* When she's not talking about her children, her house, or her husband, she's describing her banking career or her fabulous tennis game. Male Braggers often are tolerated more than women, but I find them equally annoying. They don't understand the difference between friendship and competition.

All they really want is kudos from you, so just let them have it. Fawn on about all their accomplishments, and when you're ready for them to shut up, tell them how you just love having an awful backhand because it helps all those insecure people feel better. And thank heaven for Salvation Army or your kids would be running around naked.

Life is too short to have—or to be—a bad friend. If you found yourself on the list, straighten up and fly right. And if this list reminds you of anybody you know, dump away.

Your Trash Talk is Our Wicked Pleasure

"If you can't say anything nice about somebody, come sit by me."

When Olympia Dukakis uttered this wicked line in *Steel Magnolias*, she spoke for everyone who's ever indulged in the secretive thrill of dishing.

Who doesn't enjoy hearing a little gossip?

For some reason it's delightfully wicked to hear trash talk about somebody else. And the more sordid the details, the faster it will get repeated. A neighbor's nasty divorce might make juicy fodder for the Labor Day cookout, and if an affair was involved, people will still be talking about it on New Year's Eve.

Companies struggle to communicate their corporate goals, but if someone overhears a screaming match between two VPs, it will be repeated verbatim at every meeting for years to come. The full text of the fight probably will show up on e-mail faster than you can click "send/receive all." And while I may not be able to get anybody to return my calls when I'm looking for church volunteers, if I left a message saying, "You are not going to believe what I just found out about the minister and his wife," my phone would start ringing off the hook.

We might not want to inflict emotional drama on others, but we sure want to hear about it when it happens.

The word gossip comes from the Old English *godsibb*, meaning *god sibling*, which referred to the four godparents who were present at the baptism of a child.

However, I suspect that discussing a child's spiritual development wasn't nearly as captivating to the pub crowd as chatting about how much grog the out-of-town relatives were chugging before the ceremony even began.

People have been talking trash about each other ever since the neighbors passed time during the big rainstorm by making fun of that goofy guy Noah stockpiling lumber down by the lake.

Whether it's the court jesters whispering to each other about the gluttonous, skirt-chasing antics of King Henry the VIII or today's adult-conversation-starved moms who stay late after PTA to catch the gossip—everybody wants the inside scoop. We're often so enthralled by the antics of others that we'll purposely pick the slow line at the grocery store just so we'll have time to scan the tabloids.

I used to try to pass myself off as a faux intellectual and spiritual seeker, but when I began asking my hairdresser for fifteen minutes more under the dryer just so I can find out how many plastic surgeries Cher has had, I knew the jig was up. I was just as addicted to the juicy morsels as everybody else. Now, after years of secretly pimping *People* magazine at the salon, I've come clean, and my subscription hits my mailbox every Friday afternoon. Can I really be expected to work when there's vital information about Brad, Jen, and Angelina sitting on my desk?

I'm not alone in my reading habits; four of the top ten U.S. magazines (by revenue) are tabloids: *People, National Enquirer, Star Magazine,* and *US Weekly.* My neighbor says she likes to read about celebrity gossip so she can feel informed. I often try to rationalize my own listening to personal gossip with the excuse that if I know what's going on with people, I will be able to offer better support. We can justify our actions all we like, but the moment when we get the down-and-dirty is nothing but wicked pleasure. It makes us feel both superior and in-the-know.

Gossip appeals to our inner voyeurs. And when it's really juicy, it provides a welcome diversion from the mundane matters of our own existence. But if suddenly we all started leading wildly exciting, emotionally fulfilling lives, would the *National Enquirer* go down the tubes? I doubt it. We are wired to want to know other people's business. Judging the actions of others is often how we establish our own moral compasses. And let's be honest here—going around repeating only nice stuff is kind of boring. Maybe if we all felt loved and adored for who we are, we could turn a deaf ear when somebody broadcasts the nasty news about somebody else.

But until then, perhaps we can just not take pleasure in it. If you want to dish the dirt in a nice way, I think I can make some space on the sofa—right beside me.

What's Wrong with These People?

"Can you believe she gets away with acting like that?"

"I guess Mr. Perfect thinks the rules don't apply to him."

"Who died and made her Queen of Sheba?"

We all know people who push our buttons. They don't operate by the same rules as we do, and their behavior drives us nuts. There's the self-centered brother-in-law who ignores his family and spends his weekends at the golf course or vegged out on the couch. The stuck up co-worker who brazenly barges into the boss's office demanding a raise, while the rest of us slave away in silence. Or the drama queen sister-in-law who not only rewrites the past and gets away with it, but always manages to ensnare the entire family in her movie of the week.

What's even more annoying than their irresponsible bossy, stuck-up, flighty, overly emotional, rigid, repressed, judgmental, blankety-blank ways is the fact that nobody ever calls them on the carpet for their bad behavior. So week-after-week, month-after-month, year-after-year, we watch them get away with it.

A friend of mine was lamenting how her loopy sister-in-law continues to wreak havoc on the entire family by forcing them to constantly dance around her needs and emotions. Whether it be meals, vacations, or holidays, the sister-in-law's drama was always center stage. But as I commiserated with her all-too-familiar scenario, I also sensed an undertone of the green-eyed monster at play.

"Are you jealous?" I asked.

"Jealous?" she replied, aghast. "You've got to be kidding me. Why would I ever be jealous of her? I'd never act like that."

"But doesn't it seem unfair that she gets away with it, and everybody likes her anyway?"

Bingo. Score one for the amateur shrink.

My friend's jaw dropped, and her eyes flew open wide as she exclaimed: "Oh my God, I *am* jealous. It's not fair; it seems like she's cheating, and everybody keeps validating her behavior."

In the race to win the love and respect of others, we've all got our own script of how we think people should act. Whether it's silently sweating through years of thankless work, accomplishing more than the neighbor's kids, always deferring to everybody else's needs, or expressing our feelings freely—we're convinced that there's a single template for being loved and adored. It's usually a combination of what impressed our parents most, what society reinforces, and, in my case, a little too much TV.

When someone blatantly disregards the very virtues we think of as requirements, it's maddening. And if others continue to like the offender anyway, it often feels like a slap in the face.

"How can everybody be nice to him or her when I'm over here doing things the right way, and nobody is even noticing?"

And woe to the family members who have the nerve to actually love the evil troublemaker. It's downright unfathomable that those closest to us can't see the malefactor for what she or he really is. But unfortunately the rest of the world didn't get the same memo as we did about how to prove your worth as a human being.

So, while you're fuming that your wimpy sister-in-law never steps up to the plate and embraces your boisterous family's unspoken pact that strong women are supposed to run the show, your husband's genteel brood is probably wondering when that bossy woman he married will start acting like a proper wife and keep her opinions to herself.

Someone else's failure to adhere to our personal standards is irritating, but what often hurts the most is the secret belief that if we acted like that ourselves, we would be shuttled out the back door faster than Grandma could scratch us out of her will.

Jealousy is a natural emotion when it seems like other people don't have to jump through the same hoops as we do in order to be loved, but their differences are only an affront to our virtues if we let them be.

They may be button-pushers, but they're your buttons.

2

What is the Meaning of Life & Where Did I Leave My Keys?

*"When I hear somebody sigh, 'Life is hard,'
I am always tempted to ask,
'Compared to what?'"*

—SYDNEY HARRIS

All Stressed Up and No Place to Go

The shrink test said he was motivated, creative, and flexible. Surely this thing wasn't talking about my husband.

My formerly big bucks-earning husband was starting a new chapter in his life. After twenty-three years of selling his soul to corporate America, he'd left his job and was spending quality time contemplating his true purpose in life. Part of the discovering himself process included a whole battery of shrink tests.

As I read the summary about the energetic, talkative guy who could "change directions quickly based on new information," I thought, "I can't believe it. He lied on the test!"

These tests are supposed to be foolproof, yet the person being described in the report bore little resemblance to the always tired, rather morose, "I don't want to try anything new" guy I'd been living with for eighteen years.

I wanted to be supportive; I really did. I know he has his finer qualities, but this test was way off the mark. Selfishly, though, I also knew it wouldn't be too smart to start eroding the confidence of the man who's trying to support our family.

So for once I kept my mouth shut. Instead of telling him we should get our money back for this obviously flawed report, I asked him what he thought of the results. "I think it describes me to a *T*," he said. "I'm really glad I did it."

Nodding and smiling in a nice, wifely way, I wondered, "How can a guy be so clueless about his own personality?"

And then he handed me the other report. "I didn't spend much time with this one," he said, "but it shows how I behave under stress." Ahhh. Moody, distant, withdrawn, "quits when frustrated and tends to take things too personally." Now that was my man.

As I contemplated the two reports, I had an epiphany: Maybe he really is that creative expressive guy, but he's been under so much stress over the last few years I didn't even know it.

And maybe it's not just him.

Do we ever really know anyone? Or is everybody walking around so stressed out, the personality we see on the outside has little resemblance to what lies buried within? That positive report rang true for my husband because it described what he had always known himself to be. What I had assumed was his genuine temperament—uncommunicative, grumpy, and tired—wasn't his personality at all. It was his response to twelve-hour days, heavy travel, and years of mind-numbing corporate crud.

Since he took the test, he's gotten in better shape, read some good books, and is starting a new business. He's actually turning into that positive person described in that initial report. Or rather, I should say, now that he's rid of some of the stress, that creative, exciting person he'd always been on the inside is finally opening up to the rest of the world. He's not Mr. Sunshine all the time, but I see his new personality often enough to realize it's the real him. That other guy—the stressed-out one who dragged himself through the door every night and never wanted to do anything fun—wasn't the real person. He was just a collective bunch of anxieties looking for a place to rest.

Everybody has different responses to stress, and none of them are too pretty. My husband withdraws. I prefer the control-freak reaction: tense up and start barking orders at everyone. Other people make bad jokes, talk too loud, stay silent, collapse on the bed, work too much, work too little, cry, whine, drink, or watch too much TV when they're feeling anxious.

The point is, there's often a stark contrast between the self everybody else sees and who we really are. And the more stress we're under, the greater the gap. It doesn't matter whether your stress manifests itself in being tired and grumpy or high-strung and screechy, if you act that way most of the time, people are going to assume it's your basic personality.

In hindsight, I wish I'd been more patient with my husband during his corporate years. And I wish I'd spent more time helping him deal with the situation, rather than wasting all my energy being annoyed at the way it affected him.

Funny thing about stress, once you strap on your anxiety mask, the world looks different to you and you look different to the world. It's such an effective disguise that sometimes even your own spouse doesn't recognize you.

Work-Life Balance is a Crock

Companies may love to yammer on about it, but the reality is—work-life balance is a crock.

It's a fundamentally flawed concept at best. It implies that your work is on one side of the equation, and your life is over on the other. Two opposing forces that must be carefully weighed against each other at all times. Spread enough of yourself around in equal parts, and you have the formula for success.

And we wonder why we're going nuts.

The key to a richer life isn't about maintaining the proper balance, it's about creating congruence. It's about doing work that connects with the essence of who you really are. Each of us has a contribution to make, and when our work is in alignment with our skills and talents, it doesn't take away from our lives. It adds to it.

There's a four-letter word that's the true secret of success, and it has nothing to do with balance—it's L-O-V-E. Yes, you read that right—love.

From the American Revolution to Apple Computer, love has been the cornerstone of every successful venture. Have you ever seen the look on someone's face who truly loves what they do and who loves the people they are doing it with? They shine. They shine because their work reflects who they are as a human being and because they know they're making a contribution that matters.

Love isn't some flower-child, woo-woo concept we need to pursue outside the office. Love is exactly what we need to bring into our jobs. It doesn't matter whether you're working for Procter & Gamble or the PTA, infusing your work with love delivers a better ROI (return on investment) than any other single outlay you can make.

I've worked as a business consultant for fifteen years. I know how to dissect a P&L, and I've played ball with the big boys at the top of the corporate food chain. I can promise you, if you want better results, love is the answer you're looking for.

Putting love into your work means putting your actions into context. Connecting your contribution to the big picture of your organization and the big picture of your life. It's about paying attention to the moment you're in and being fully present for the people you're with. Love happens when you get your mind, your body, and your spirit in the same place at the same time. Because when you're fully present, that's when you finally give your soul permission to show up. And it's your soul that gives off the shine.

If you're mindlessly going through the motions in a job you hate, your life is on the fast track to misery, no matter how you balance it. But before you start checking the want ads, let me tell you, the meaning you get out of your work is in direct proportion to the meaning you put into it. Whether you're a volunteer or a vice president, you're the one that decides whether or not you're going to bring love into the equation.

Going to work shouldn't dim your light; it ought to ignite it. So forget balance. Start with love and think congruence, connection, and contribution instead. Monday is a new day, and it's Take Your Soul to Work Day. Because, quite frankly, I think a few of us have been leaving ours at home.

So the next time that alarm clock goes off, make the decision to wake up, show up, and shine.

The Meaning of Life in Two Words

Friendship and creativity. Who would have thought a geeky professor of quantum physics could sum up life's big question in two words? But the second I heard him say it, I knew he was right. It's one of those great ideas like disposable diapers, TIVO, and the theory of evolution. It makes sense the first time you hear it, and the more you think about it, the more you wonder why nobody ever thought of it before.

In this case, the words themselves came from Dr. Casey Blood, a rather brilliant gentleman who spends long hours contemplating the cosmos and other scientific concepts I can't even begin to understand. But the truism of his words applies to regular everyday life.

We're put on this earth to learn how to connect with each other and to use talents to create something wonderful. Our deepest desire is to be cherished while on this planet and to make a contribution that outlasts our stay on it. The concept is simple; it's the execution that's hard, and the biggest challenge is all those other crazy human beings who want the same thing. They plague us with their unrelenting demands; they don't love us the way we'd like; and they insist on inserting their own quirks, ideas, and dysfunctions into our plans.

Ahh, if only they would see things our way, the world would be a perfect place indeed.

Friendship and creativity are relatively straightforward words, but the full context of their meanings can be huge.

True friendship isn't just mindless chit-chat around the water cooler. It stands for love, acceptance, and unconditional support. Who doesn't want more of that in every relationship?

And while we might think that creativity only applies to the whiz kid at the ad agency or the annoying mime pestering you at the street fair, it's actually the core of any meaningful contribution.

Every task offers an opportunity to create. Whether you're a painter, publicist, or parent, your life's work is your legacy. And whether you do it with your hands, your mind, or your heart, creativity ultimately expands when you have the help of others.

Yet that's where the conflict comes in. The difference between the idea of friendship and creativity and their execution is a little like the difference between dating and marriage. And I'm guessing I'm not the only person who was better at one of those than the other.

In a perfect world our relationships would stimulate creativity, and creating together would deepen our relationships. But in the real world, we often lack the time and patience to work through the process.

Who hasn't found themselves thinking, "This project would go quicker if that annoying so-and-so weren't involved?" And I can't tell you how many times I've been convinced my household would run more smoothly if my husband would just adhere to my edicts. Alas, such is the nature of the human ego. Our souls want to be part of something bigger than ourselves, but our egos keep telling us those other people are standing in the way.

Enter the cheap, no-work, pop culture solutions—TV and

shopping. We can create, we can connect, and we never have to put up with real people.

Want to experience the satisfaction of pulling together something great? Forget toiling over a communal garden or cranking out a big, multi-department project. You can surround yourself with artsy furniture or get a fab, new outfit today. Craving some witty repartee? Ditch your family with all their boring woes. Get TIVO and the *Friends* down at the coffee shop will rerun their funny lines forever. Invest in a big screen and Jennifer Aniston becomes nearly life size. Or as life size as a size 2 gets.

The beauty and the curse of television is that it satisfies our desire for intimacy with no emotional work or responsibility on our part. And consumerism feeds off our need for a creative outlet.

I'm no earth mother. I've got a closet full of shoes, and I can recite the scripts of almost every *Brady Bunch* episode since Mike and Carol married. But I also know the deeper meaning we crave can't be found in pop culture solutions. Discovering your true purpose isn't always easy. It takes intention and the discipline to turn away from the quick fixes being marketed to the masses. You're also going to have to make an emotional investment in the people around you.

TV and shopping aren't cheap substitutes for the real thing. They're expensive ones. You deserve the real deal— friendship and creativity. It's really that simple. And it's really that hard.

3

Why Do Men Resist Change & Why Do Women Bother to Try?

"Do we have to talk about this right now?
My nachos are almost ready."

—BOB MCLEOD

Take a Wife and Call Me in the Morning

Medical science and country music agree—the love of a good woman does in fact make him a better man.

Science has long proven that married men are healthier, live longer, and make more money. And the "she makes me want to be a better man" theme has been a staple of Nashville gold long before Johnny Cash sang, "Because you're mine, I walk the line."

But while a woman may make a man want to be better and while medical science may prove that she actually does, how many men enthusiastically participate in their improvement process?

My own dear husband has been attending the "Lisa McLeod School of Personal Development" for more than twenty years, having won a full scholarship the day we got married. However, I'm beginning to think that despite the weekly (oh, all right, daily) lectures from the Institute's lead instructor, he's not enjoying this enlightening experience. The diverse curriculum covers everything from diet and exercise to parenting and painting skills, yet he remains a completely uninspired student.

Perhaps he doesn't understand the science behind this educational endeavor.

In the *Parade Magazine* cover story, "Why Marriage Is Good Medicine for Men," author Gail Sheehy suggests that women improve their men's lives, specifically their health and longevity, because "left to their own devices and vices, men are inattentive to physical symptoms." Women typically act as "the health sentries" for men. Any woman who's ever argued with her husband about the merits of convenience store nachos knows that men don't typically troll the vegetable aisle on their own. Although I now feel totally vindicated in my quest to eliminate deep fried pork rinds from my man's diet, the article also states that a wife's loving touch and regular sex are the most essential elements in determining a man's emotional and physical health.

Groan—as if I don't have enough to do.

It turns out that it's not just being married that makes a man healthy, wealthy, and wise; it's being *happily* married. And for men, happy means lots of caresses, unconditional support, and plenty of time in the sack.

"When all is said and done," writes Sheehy, "a solid marriage with regular, enthusiastic sex can be the best preventative medicine of all."

In fact, a decade-long study at Queen's University in Belfast about the mortality of middle-aged men revealed that men who had sex three or more times a week had a fifty percent reduced risk of heart attack or stroke. So technically speaking, whenever your husband says, "I'll die if I don't have more sex," he's actually right. I'm surprised that every man in America doesn't have this study encoded in his e-mail signature.

Like it or not, the science is clear: Men benefit in numerous ways from the loving attention of a wife.

Blogger and gender studies professor Hugo Schwyzer (HugoBoy.typepad.com) goes so far as to say, "Marriage, done right, strips away a man's selfishness and self-absorption like nothing else."

That may be true, but here's where the country music part comes in. A man may love being inspired by a woman, but he doesn't want the rules enforced by one. As country crooner Keith Urban sings, "When you put your arms around me, you let me know there's nothing I can't do," the operative word here being *I*. He didn't say, "There's nothing you can't make me do."

There's a fine line between nudging and nagging. The longer you've been married and the busier you are, the easier it is for a wife to cross it.

But the singers and the scientists concur: Behind every healthy, successful man is a good woman holding him up.

Now, if only I had the energy and patience to become one.

Wine, Roses, Mittens: It Must Be Love

Of all the stupid products designed to henpeck men, I have just discovered the worst: The Smitten, a hideous gift marketed for Valentine's Day.

The Smitten set consists of a left mitten, a right mitten, and a mitten for two. According to the ad, the heart-shaped mitten with two cuffs allows "you and your honey to hold hands tenderly and warmly while braving the outdoors." Pass me a barf bag. A fluffy, red mitten for two? I wouldn't want to be seen in public with the man who would wear this. You might as well put him on a pink, sparkly leash and be done with it.

What I want to know is, what happens if you trip while your hands are stuck inside this thing? I guess the googly-eyed Romeo, who willingly attaches himself to you under a red heart of "warm plush polar fleece," isn't too worried about having his hands free in the event of an emergency. Even the guy in the ad (Smitten.com) looks embarrassed to be wearing it.

If ever there is a time when the differing male/female versions of romance collide, it's on Valentine's Day. Women think the gift giving is supposed to last all month—or at the very least, consist of multiple, carefully chosen items on the big day.

Men, on the other hand, often don't remember the holiday until they're on their way home from work on the fourteenth. The Gas 'N Go may offer a lovely display of chocolates, but we women know that if the guy really loves you, he starts composing his sonnet right after Christmas.

The lengths we'll go to turn a macho man into simpering sap are just amazing.

We all know the drill: We're attracted to men, and then after they commit to us, we try to make them act like women. Whether it was his strong, silent demeanor or his slightly unkempt, rugged looks, whatever first drew us in is the first thing we try to change once our blinding hormones wear off.

Yet if you could actually change a man, a job many women braver than you have tried and failed, I doubt you would be happy with the result.

Relationship expert and TV commentator Lisa Daily, (LisaDaily.com) says, "Men need to be men, and bless them for that. The very same brain cells that prevent him from wearing matching sweatshirts are also the ones that cause him to give you his coat when it gets chilly outside, or kill the really big, nasty bug in your kitchen. These are good brain cells."

Testosterone may be great for growing back hair, but it's not going to make a man start dotting his *i*'s with little hearts. The reality is that if a guy grew you a room full of roses, called you every hour, and smothered you with cutesy stuffed animals, you probably wouldn't find him very interesting.

Men are programmed to do the wooing, but it works best when they get to choose their tools. Instead of trying to make a man conform to your ideas of romance, give him some room to create his own.

Turned-down pages in a catalog strategically placed on the back of the commode don't make anybody feel dreamy. Smothering a man in The Smitten may keep your hands warm. But the guy who insists on choosing his own gloves is the one who can really make your palms sweat.

Why Must I Always Be Grateful?

Don't you just love it when your big, strong man helps you out? Doing special little favors like cooking meals for the

family, cleaning up after the dog, and babysitting HIS OWN
CHILDREN! (Insert rolling eyes here.)

Why is it that when a man does something around the
house, he sees it as "helping" his wife and believes he needs
to be thanked for his efforts? This happens in spite of the
fact that on the previous 997 occasions, his wife washed the
clothes or fed the kids with nary a peep of gratitude from
anyone, let alone him.

I know there are plenty of exceptions. My own dear husband is a true co-parent who does not consider watching his
own flesh and blood a charitable action on my behalf. But
if the two of us spend the day cleaning out the basement,
I'm supposed to thank God on bended knee that my man
"helped me out."

The nice part of my brain knows that praising a man for
his efforts makes him feel wonderful and will motivate him to
do even more. But sometimes my evil twin wants to scream,
"Why should I have to bat my eyes and say 'Thank you, you
big ole hunk o' man,' every time you get off the couch?! If
anybody should be thanked it's me, for my uncanny ability
to recognize what needs to be done."

Professor Jay Belsky of the Institute for the Study of Children, Families, and Social Issues at Birbeck University of
London has discovered one of the big reasons why men and
women have such different attitudes about household work.

Belsky's research revealed that while men typically measure their contributions around the house against what their
fathers did, a woman measures her husband's efforts against
what she is doing.

In his book, *The Transition to Parenthood: How a First
Child Changes a Marriage*, Belsky explains that a man doing

thirty percent of the household chores, whose father only did ten percent, feels like he's performing 300 percent, because he's doing three times more than his dad ever did.

But his wife, who takes care of the other seventy percent, thinks he's not even making a half-hearted effort, because his thirty percent is still less than half of what she's doing.

And if she has to nag him to get it done and shower him with flower petals when he's finished, she knocks off even more percentage points.

My husband takes a less scientific approach. In choosing to speak for his entire gender, he explains why men always expect their wife to say thank you, even if the job the man did is something that benefits the entire family, himself included. He says, "The woman is the queen of the house. It's her kingdom. And when I do favors for the queen there should be restitution."

If scrubbing the toilet qualifies a man for knighthood, then cleaning up the cat pee must make him feel like he deserves the crown jewels. If you've been married a while, you probably also know there are a few other little gems most men consider more than adequate compensation for their heroic efforts around the house.

A woman might not make the connection between her man painting the bedroom and then getting to spend more time in it, but a man sure does.

The good news is, it doesn't take much to make a man feel appreciated. The bad news is most women resent the heck out of doing it. If your husband cleans out the pantry while you're getting your nails done, it's easy to be gracious. But when he pitches in and simply matches your efforts, it's hard to understand why you owe him.

Women often feel that our bar is set at 100 percent of the tasks while the male bar rests at zero and that any deviation off those preset marks is something we're supposed to be grateful for.

But I suspect for all the annoyed women, there's a pack of equally frustrated men who are trying their best and are completely baffled about why their wives respond with, "Don't expect any medals from me," instead of, "Thank you." If you're a guy, there's a simple solution to this problem: Do more without being asked, and when you're done, tell her the difficulty of the task really made you appreciate how much work she puts in for your family.

And if you're a woman, your solution is even easier: Say thank you. You've probably faked other stuff in your life before, so faking gratitude shouldn't be too big of a leap for you. And who knows? Sometimes you start off faking it, but after doing it for a while, you actually start to enjoy it.

The Secret Angst of Men, Imposters Within
"Why do you have to question everything I do?"

If there's a non-defensive guy out there who enjoys his wife asking him questions, I'd sure like to meet him. And if there's a woman who successfully has mastered the art of asking her husband a question about something he's done without him interpreting it as nagging or insulting, get yourself to the phone, call Oprah, and start sharing your secret on TV. Right now. Because, aside from the option of spending my entire marriage bound and gagged—something I suspect my better half has secretly wished for a few times—I have yet to figure out this gender dynamic.

I've long known that men interpret the female tendency

to ask lots of questions as demeaning. I've watched plenty of guys, including my own husband, hear an innocent question from their wives or colleagues and mentally attach, "You stupid idiot, can't I trust you with anything?" to the end of it.

Yet despite twenty years of marriage and a lifetime of corporate work, I never fully understood the deep and often painful roots of this bewildering aspect of male behavior—until now.

In an eye-opening book, *For Women Only*, author Shaunti Feldhahn reveals what's really going on in the minds of men. Based on spoken and written interviews with more than 1,000 men, Feldhahn exposes revelations about men that surprised the heck out of me. Many were things I thought I knew, like how much sex matters to a man, how much they want to be respected, and why they feel a need to provide.

But reading the actual words of men helped me see the depth of male feelings—yes, they do have them—behind these surface assumptions. Much like Feldhahn, I was shocked to learn what's really going on in the inner lives of men.

One of the biggest surprises was how many men feel like frauds. Feldhahn writes, "Despite their in-control exteriors, men often feel like imposters and are insecure that their inadequacies will be discovered." Apparently, they're all secretly afraid somebody is going to find them out.

Feldhahn's research (available at 4-womenonly.com) reveals that "a man's vulnerability about his performance (in everything) often stems from his conviction that at all times he is being watched and judged."

You'd probably get defensive too if you thought the world was always waiting for you to make a mistake.

Another startling insight was learning that most men face

a constant battle with ever-present sexual images fighting for attention inside their heads. I've always known men were stimulated by visual images, but according to Feldhahn's surveys, it's not just pimple-faced sixteen-year-olds whose fantasies of Beyonce keep them distracted in algebra. Most grown men are walking around with a huge visual Rolodex of women, she says, and it takes a massive effort to ignore it.

Feldhahn's interviews included large numbers of church-going men whom she personally knew to be nice, normal, loving husbands. Yet she discovered that "even happily married men struggle with being pulled into live and recollected images of other women."

As I read about the secret inner lives of men, my emotions jumped between sympathy, sorrow, and anger. I felt sympathetic because it must be pretty hard to function when you feel like everyone's judging you, and every time you turn around, the image of a naked woman flashes through your brain. I was saddened that men often are so misunderstood. And I was angry that none of the men in my life ever bothered to clue me in about all this inner angst. The biggest shocker of the book was how surprised men were to discover that we women didn't already know those things about them.

I was getting good and annoyed thinking, "Isn't that just like a bunch of men to tell a surveyor something they never bothered to share with their own wives?" But then I came to the last question.

"What is the one thing you wish your wife or significant other knew, but you feel you can't explain or tell her?"

The majority of men said, "How much I love her."

4

Can You Become CEO by Standing Next to the Water Cooler?

"By the time he's finished
he will have fired everyone around him…
and poor Donald will be sitting there
on his little pedestal all by himself "

—MARTHA STEWART ON DONALD TRUMP

Chumps or Chimps: Monkeys in the Middle of Management

Does your boss remind you of an ape?

Snorting around, grunting orders, lurching through the office with his knuckles dragging the ground. Beating his chest and growling every five minutes just to prove to all the other primates that he's Chief Chimp in Charge. Turns out gorilla bosses have more in common with their grub-eating counterparts than we ever thought. And it's more than just a hairy back.

Neurobiology research reveals there are significant parallels between the brain activity of workplace bullies and that of chest-thumping gorillas.

The cerebral, "thinking" part of the human brain has evolved into a sophisticated mechanism that operates on multiple dimensions. But science has shown that our big modern brains actually grew over a more primitive limbic brain, an instinct-driven, survivalist-oriented system that closely resembles that of an ape.

So while your boss may display a thin veneer of humanity in front of higher-ups and customers, buried beneath his (or her) fancy car, cushy office, and endless PowerPoint presentations is the mind of a monkey.

And it's the monkey mind that takes over in times of stress or when there's no fear of reprisal.

"The need to dominate, intimidate, and oppress has its basis in an innate, instinctual, primitive need," suggests business owner and psychology writer David Weiner, author of *Power Freaks: Dealing With Them in the Workplace or Anyplace.*

That explains why your manager thinks banging on the glass and grunting at you is appropriate behavior for the workplace. And why, if all the other big silverbacks get transferred to cushy jobs back at the home office in Dayton, your boss charges around the office, throwing branches and rocks at all the underlings in a futile attempt to defend his dominance.

Weiner explains how ape-like behaviors manifest in the workplace. "The primitive brain mechanism drives us into creating hierarchies (promotions, executive perks, bonuses and salary ladders) and defending our territory (corner office, best parking spot, taking credit for the success of a group-generated project), two behaviors essential for primitive organization and survival," he writes.

As a species that shares 98.5 percent of its DNA with chimps, it should be no surprise that the modern workplace—with its cubicles and organization trees—is merely a fancied-up version of *Planet of the Apes.*

And since the limbic brain instinctively connects status to survival, ambitious primates often will do anything to maintain control of the tire swing. According to Weiner, "Tension to move up the ranks or defend one's position exists innately within our instinctual-emotional minds and is activated when we sense an opportunity for advancement or we receive a challenge from someone attempting to displace us."

As a former Fortune 500 flunky myself, I've spent a little time observing the monkey-see, monkey-do dance called corporate America. And I can promise you that in the race to become top banana, the inner chimp often takes over, and all the other monkeys get shoved down the vine.

According to Weiner and other scientists, the neurotransmitter serotonin is usually to blame. "When tested, the people you suspect (CEOs, sports stars, and overly ambitious middle managers) have richer serotonin levels than everyone else. And once your level goes up your outlook is permanently skewed," Weiner says.

Weiner, also the author of *Conquering your Inner Dummy,* says the link between serotonin and social dominance explains why some primates stay on top while others are doomed to the back of the cage forever.

Testosterone also plays a role. Winning the big game, snagging the big account, or being voted Grand Pooba of the lodge boosts testosterone. But while the winners are jumping around, beating their chests, and chattering on about how great they are, scientists can track negative changes in the neurons of higher animals after a "social defeat."

Those on top often believe it's their God-given right to be there and that the lesser apes only exist to peel their fruit.

Lest you think power-freak behavior is limited to men, remember the famous Queen of Mean, Leona Helmsley, who notoriously belittled employees and whose outrageous power trip ultimately landed her in jail.

Weiner says the results of the limbic power quiz on his web site (BrainTricks.com) indicate women are just as likely to be power freaks as men. So while the president of the PTA may have better hair than Donald Trump, she may be just as capable of gleefully ordering lesser monkeys to fetch her another kumquat.

Next time your boss goes ape, just smile and remember: You don't have to be Tarzan to live happily amongst the chimps.

Now strap on that monkey suit and get back to work.

Power Lunching 101: A High Stakes Test of Humanity

A red cup placed at the head of your table means no talking; a green cup means polite conversation with your immediate neighbor. Such are the rules of elementary school lunches where discipline is the goal and lunchroom monitors have the power to take away your socializing privileges for the slightest infraction.

Times have changed, and in an era where standardized testing reigns supreme, lunchroom conduct is evaluated on a daily basis. Getting milk to squirt out of your nose may still elicit a big hee-haw from your friends, but you're also going to get a check mark in your folder, and your class will be put on red cup faster than you can say "social outcast."

I understand the school's need for crowd control. Getting a thousand hungry kids in and out of a lunchroom in less than two hours is a mission that would have challenged Gen. Patton. Most of the educators I know are incredibly committed to the cause. Despite being lorded over by folks who never set foot in a classroom, they continue to do the best they can with what they've got.

The real issue isn't teachers or individual school systems. They're just operating within the parameters they've been given; the bigger question is—what do we really want our kids to learn? The three *R*'s is an easy answer. Teach them to read, tell them to write, assign lots of math problems, and test them at every step along the way to make sure they're getting it. Hold teachers accountable based on the results, and eventually our kids will rule the world.

But how many CEOs, world leaders, or acclaimed humanitarians achieved success because of their high SAT scores? The people who do really well in life are the ones who know how to connect with others. The engineers who make partner are the ones who work well with clients; the scientists who get to run the departments are the ones with good management skills; and the hairdressers who make the big bucks are those who listen and provide witty repartee along with well-placed highlights to cover your gray. Excellent technical skills can carry you to the middle, but influencing others is what takes you to the top.

Dr. Rebecca Parker, the noted Unitarian Universalist and

president of Star King School for the Ministry, suggests that a true education "allows the time and space for the student's mind to unfold."

I don't know about you, but I didn't figure out what I was good at until my mid thirties. Hour after hour spent writing, "I will not talk at lunch," on the blackboard appears to have done me no good whatsoever, but conversing with my friends and exposure to new ideas ignited my mind in a way that rigid discipline and rote memorization never could.

Good teachers don't try to mold—they help with the unfolding. And interpersonal skills are a huge part of the equation. My children have been blessed with several truly gifted teachers who taught the subject matter required and helped the students develop their social skills at the same time. They didn't leave any child behind because they created classroom communities that worked together to move everybody ahead. That relaxed, back-and-forth communication can't happen when kids have their heads bent over a high-stakes bubble test.

Shoving endless academic knowledge and skills down our kids' throats may bump up their spots on the bell curve, but they're not going to be any happier or more successful unless they learn how to manage their personal lives.

An inability to do fractions can't suck the life out of you the way bad relationships and lack of social support can. And the Corporate Corridor of Cubicles is littered with the bodies of junior executives who failed Power Lunching 101.

So put down your pencils, look up from your books, and yack away. You're on green cup, kids, and this *will* be on the test.

Are Friends Vital to Your Paycheck?

Want to skyrocket to the top of the corporate food chain? Forget trying to bribe your boss with a cheese log. If you really want to get promoted, you need a best friend.

Late night e-mails, dazzling Power Points, and volunteering to create a three-inch binder documenting the work of your cross-functional, multi-department synergistic project team may seem like the fast track to the corner office, but new research reveals that having a best friend at work can boost your career even faster than kissing up to the boss.

An extensive workplace study from Gallup reveals that people who have a best friend at work are significantly more likely to get more done in less time, have fun on the job, innovate and share ideas, and have a safe workplace with fewer accidents.

Kind of confirms why you may have been happier waiting tables with your college buddies than you are knocking back the big bucks alone in your corporate cube.

But merely having *a* friend at work isn't enough. Those generic "Good morning," mindless chit-chat office mates— the ones we call "friends" but who are actually mere acquaintances we'll never see again after we leave our job— have no effect on our productivity whatsoever.

But if you're lucky enough to have a "best friend" at work, you're seven times more likely to be engaged in your job. Unfortunately, out of the 8 million people surveyed by Gallup, only thirty percent of employees report having a close, supportive confidant at work.

Best-selling author Tom Rath uses the research to make a compelling case for friendship in his latest book, *Vital Friends: The People You Can't Afford to Live Without.* He says, "When you think about your best job, it always goes back to the relationships, the local work group, or the local manager."

In fact, the Gallup research indicates that "close friendships at work can increase your satisfaction with your organization by fifty percent" and "double your chances of having a favorable perception of your pay."

Good grief. If all it takes is a few friends to make you happy with your comp plan, you'd think every boss in America would be sending their staff out for margaritas every Friday afternoon. However, Rath, the head of Gallup's Workplace Research and Leadership Consulting arm, says, "Most companies don't do much to help people build relationships." Managers are afraid that "if the employees get together, they'll be talking about me."

If you're a jerk boss, we probably are trashing you at the Christmas party you made us pay for ourselves.

Rath reports, "Close workplace friendships are consistently one of the best predictors of an organization's profitability," but when companies discourage employee fraternization, people become "belly-ache buddies based on their mutual hatred of their employer."

As someone who once spent hours with her co-workers plotting our plan to publicly expose our evil, alcoholic, sexually harassing boss, I can promise you, mutual moaning isn't nearly as much fun as doing worthwhile work with your pals. I've preached about the value of friendship for years, but after a decade in the seminar biz, I have yet to see a company pay for a "how to be a better friend" workshop. As Rath insightfully points out, "The energy between two people is what creates great marriages, families, teams, and organizations. Yet when we think consciously about improving our lives, we put almost all of our efforts into self-development."

Bogus rah-rah programs to improve company loyalty fail time and time again; however, loyalty between employees has been at the root of every vibrant, successful organization since the dawn of time.

You can learn more about the study and take the friendship quiz at VitalFriends.com

But in the meantime, skip that time management seminar and start chatting it up with your pals at the water cooler and idling away your hours gossiping in the company cafeteria. And if your boss happens to catch you, you can honestly say, "Hey, I'm working here."

5

How Did My Woo-Woo Get So
Out of Wack?

*"Housework, if you do it right,
will kill you."*

—ERMA BOMBECK

Leftover Pizza Boxes, Hold the Chi

My chi is stuck.

My karmic flow of good energy is wedged somewhere between a pile of half-naked Barbies and thirty-seven old newspapers.

Lodged between all the magazines I've been meaning to read, the kids' craft clutter, and two permission slips I forgot to sign, lies the power of the universe, and it's being strangled by my computer cords and old, mismatched socks.

I had a feng shui consultant visit my home recently, and she confirmed what I have long suspected: Clutter is sucking the life force from our family. We are literally drowning in a black hole of junk.

As she went from room to room—or rather, I should say, from pile to pile—feng shui consultant Katharine Deleot tactfully suggested that parting with some of our assorted stuff might make life a bit simpler.

"One of the principles of feng shui," she said, "is that we want to be in a good and current relationship with our stuff." I'm guessing that's a nice way of saying, "How can you people even function with all that crap on your kitchen counter?"

"But it's not me!" I wanted to scream. "It's the kids!" Those little devils bring in plastic parts by the boatload. Every time I turn around, it's a homework paper here, seventy-three little counting beads there, and a visual montage of the life of a moth strewn across the dining room table.

And the party bags—ugh. Why does everyone seem to think my kids need to leave every event they attend toting plastic necklaces and a magnetic tic-tac-toe game? Talk about trinkets and trash. Between birthday parties, school give-aways, and visits to Grandma's house, my kids bring home more booty than an accountant grabbing free pens at a trade show.

But as much as I tried to lay the blame on my poor, defenseless children, when we got to my office, there was no denying the obvious: The Queen of Clutter was actually me. Papers were piled high on the desk, and there were enough electrical cords to choke an entire Chinese village.

Deleot says everyone has a "clutter quotient." Ever the over-achiever, mine is quite high, it appears. But as Deleot diplomatically pointed out, "When your clutter starts depleting your energy, it's blocking the flow of your life."

Author Karen Rauch Carter (FengShuiPalace.com) defines *feng shui* (pronounced fung shway) as "purposefully arranging the stuff around you to gain positive results."

Donald Trump incorporated feng shui principles into

the Trump World Tower, and Disney made sure the chi was flowing when it built Hong Kong Disneyland.

Deleot says: "Chi is the essential energy that connects all living things. It flows like water, and clutter is like stones in the river; it blocks the flow of energy from supporting you. Feng shui aims to design and arrange environments to harmonize and balance the flow."

So, together, we tried to get my office (and hopefully me) in better harmony. My desk is now facing the power position—the best view of the room and the door. I'm getting one of those cool little water gardens to put in the creativity section. And I've written a job description for my dream PR intern and placed it in the helpful people corner.

I'm shocked at what a difference it's made. I feel better, and I'm actually more productive.

But the endless piles of the papers, or wood energy, as they're referred to in feng shui, are still the bane of my existence. The Buddha might have been able to organize all his personal papers in a small, carved wood box, but his accountant wasn't nagging at him to keep seven years of tax returns.

Yet, slowly but surely, piece by piece, I'm getting my clutter-choked chi flowing. I only hope that once it starts to move, it doesn't take my phone bill with it.

Leaping Through Life Turns You into a Toad
If you drop a frog in a pot of boiling water, it will immediately leap out. But if you put a frog in cool water and gradually turn up the heat, the frog will boil to death without ever trying to escape.

The same thing happens to people.

If someone had told you ten years ago that one day your life would include three events in a single evening, thirty-two rounds of cell phone tag, and fifty-seven emails waiting for you when you got home, you would have jumped out of that kettle faster than you can say "deep-fried frog legs."

But just like the amphibian that starts off in lukewarm water, the pace of your life often heats up so gradually you aren't even aware of the fire.

You add one thing, then another, then another. And while each individual activity may be worthwhile, or even fun, the collective total makes you feel like you're thrashing around in a hot pot 24/7. And no amount of time management skills will make the water stop boiling.

Want a surefire way to turn an enjoyable event into total misery? Try packing it in with three other things on the same day and leaving yourself only five minutes to get from one stop to the next. And if you really want to turn the whole day into slow, draining torture, drag a few kids along with you.

Working a two-hour stint in the prize booth at my kids' Spring Fling provided an up-close glimpse of the price we pay for the "we're going to get all this stuff done if it kills us" syndrome.

For those of you unfamiliar with the Fling phenomenon, imagine kids hurling beanbags through the mouth of a big plywood clown, pink glitter butterflies painstakingly painted on snow cone-stained faces, and junk food galore. What really gets flung at a fling is lots of money—laid down by weary, well-intended parents in the hopes that their kiddos will have a good time and the school will raise enough money to pay for a new gym floor.

As head prize-booth monitor, my job was to assist the

kids as they traded in their hard-won tokens for cheap plastic prizes. I was the last stop on the Spring Fling parade of fun and after tossing enough rings over a Coke bottle to rack up a handful of tokens, the kids were more than eager to claim their bounty.

You'd think after spending hours plunking down wads of cash for the pleasure of watching their kids jump around in the Bouncy House and try to throw Ping-Pong balls into a fishbowl, the parents would be taking a break in the back of the room while their children vacillated between getting the inflatable globe or the 3-D glasses. But, no, every parent there was trying to shuttle his or her kid through as fast as possible, so they could move on to something else. Whether it was rushing off to soccer pictures or trying to get home before the icing on the cake-walk cake melted, "Hurry up, honey, we've got to go!" was the refrain of the day.

The sad part of this whole scenario was that these parents had gone to a huge amount of work to set this thing up, and they'd spent their time and money to take their kids to the event, but they were so worried about moving on to the next thing, nobody was having any fun.

Many of us have bought into the notion that proper time management is the key to a happy and balanced life. Better scheduling means more things checked off on the list, and who wouldn't be happier about that? But the overanxious, clock-watching parents at the Spring Fling were proof that if you take a bunch of fun things and cram them all together in one day, they will cease to be fun. I'm all for making the most of what you've got, but at a certain point, adding more stuff to your list diminishes the likelihood of enjoying any of it. It doesn't matter whether it's a career opportunity or T-ball game, when you schedule a zillion things in a row, your mind is so focused on frantically checking things off your list, you never fully engage in any of it.

Frogs may have a brain the size of a pea, but they're smart enough to give themselves some lily pad time in between their rounds of making tadpoles and flicking their tongues out for flies.

Next time you're tempted to throw one more event into the hopper, remember the boiling point can sneak up on you slowly. Throwing more into the pot doesn't always add to your life—sometimes it just makes you want to croak.

Put Down the Pledge and Slowly Back Away from the Coffee Table

Nothing is more annoying than a neat-nick, always out there extolling the virtues of living dirt- and dust-free.

And if the clean freaks aren't enough to make you crazy, the organizational police are even worse—you know, those lunatics who think you should only handle a piece of paper once and then know exactly where it went.

Oh, please, as if digging through the trash can, looking for your insurance bill is a bad thing. I've always been suspicious of people with no mounds of paper on their kitchen counters. Do they not get any mail? When it comes to domestic duties, most of us tend to fall into one of two camps: those who can't stand to see a job undone and those who can't stand to do it.

While no one in her right mind likes to clean a toilet and even fewer people want to use a dirty one, one of those two activities is probably more loathsome to you than the other. Being a woman with an extremely high tolerance for dirt, I'd be more likely to whip out a paper seat cover in my own home than to risk breaking a nail reaching for a scrub brush.

I've defended my sloppy ways for years and successfully thwarted all efforts to turn me into a domestic drone, but I'm beginning to wonder if all those organized people know something about life management I don't. After all, they can lay their hands on their kids' birth certificates. They don't have to shove their unsorted mail into the dryer before guests arrive. They haven't washed the same sweater three times just because it never made it out of the hamper. If only they weren't so damn self-righteous I might be tempted to emulate their ways.

As someone who fancies herself as a creative type, I've always believed boring chores and rigid routines were stifling to say the least. After all, how can you think about anything interesting when you're worried about how many more minutes your whites need to soak?

And as the author of the previous book, *Forget Perfect*, I've made it my personal mission to free women from the bondage of housework. But the irony of not being able to find a pen to jot down my latest rant against housekeeping is not lost on me.

When it comes to the "do you clean your house or don't you" question, I think many of us are missing the point. It's not about whether or not you clean—it's about why. When many people talk about the need to clean, they're often worried about the impression their house is making on others. As in, "I can't have Aunt Myra over because toys are all over the floor." Or, "We can't have a party until we get new carpet."

Truth be told, letting others see your messy house actually makes people feel better about their own piles of crud back home. So if you're cleaning or feeling guilty about not cleaning because of what the neighbors think, get over it. And if you think a spit-shined house means you're a better mother, I can promise you nothing could be further from the truth. I can't tell you how many women I've met who are so worried about their houses, they can't enjoy their kids.

Cleaning to meet the standards of others makes no sense whatsoever. If you can't relax until your house looks perfect, you're never going to get any sleep at all. However, I can also tell you from firsthand experience, living your life in a disorderly mess costs you plenty in terms of time and trouble. Having to buy three bar mitzvah cards for your nephew because you're constantly misplacing them before they get sent is hardly an efficient effort. And while too much cleaning and organizing may feel like indentured servitude, looking all over the house for your keys doesn't feel like freedom either.

I think the secret to creating bliss in your home lies in prioritizing yourself above your stuff. If cleaning up something or filing it away makes things easier for you in the long run, create a system that enables you to do it. But if you think life will finally improve once you get rid of your dust bunnies, you might want to rethink your efforts.

For me, a functional house means living with soap scum but knowing where I can find my tax return. Maybe in my next life I'll have color-coded files, cute little bins for all personal items, and all my soups lined up in alphabetical order.

But for now, until I learn to be the good example of tidiness, I'll just have to be the horrible warning for the dark and dirty side.

Hey, Buddy, Can You Spare Some Jing?

My jing is out of bling. And no amount of Doritos and NoDoz can bring it back.

I thought I had unblocked the energies of the divine when the feng shui consultant helped me clear out the clutter that was choking my chi. But just when I thought I was doing great in the woo-woo department, I discovered that my jing was gone.

Jing, defined in Chinese medicine as "the substance that underlies all organic life," is thought of as an invisible, supportive, life essence that nourishes, fuels, and cools the body. And mine isn't just blocked—it's gone! As in zapped, nada, never to return to me in this lifetime.

According to ancient Chinese wisdom, one is born with a finite amount of jing. We draw on it during our lives as an energy reserve, but once it's gone, it never comes back.

So while I was out there giving seminars for sales people who couldn't care less and staying up late ruminating about my in-laws, I was burning through my jing so fast I'm surprised my aura wasn't giving off smoke.

Even worse, once you've used up your lifetime allotment, your body is totally dependent on food, sleep, exercise, and, uggh, meditation for energy. But the everyday jing produced by a healthy lifestyle doesn't have the same staying power as the blessed birthright dose you squandered worrying about which wallpaper would work best in the master bath.

While you may be able to power through a day on Almond Joys and Diet Coke, if you're jing-less like me, the next day you'll find yourself laid out flat without enough energy to even watch the soaps.

My verdict was this: All your reserves are gone; you're just going to have to start taking care of yourself if you want to have enough energy to stand erect, make toast, or apply lip gloss. This distressing diagnosis was confirmed by a tarot card reader, so it's not like I'm making this stuff up.

When I think of all the ways I wasted my precious jing, I want to cry, but I don't have the energy to well up tears. Bad boyfriends probably sucked away a good twenty-five per-cent. Idiot bosses siphoned off another thirty. And a decade spent selling people stuff they didn't need probably robbed me of another fifteen. Maybe I should start sending out jing invoices to everybody I squandered my mojo on.

But in the end, the ultimate decider of how I spent my time was me. As much as I'd hate to see a pie chart breakdown of all the times I tapped into my inner reserves for something that didn't matter, I was the one who emptied my allotment.

What with all the late nights I powered through pre-sentation prep, the endless Saturdays spent hawking raffle tickets, and the redeye flights I took for meetings that didn't matter—I bet I only spent about ten percent of my jing on anything important, like listening to my grandmother repeat the deviled-egg story, comforting a friend through a nasty divorce, or holding the barf bucket for my kids when they had the flu.

A minister friend of mine once said, "It's a lot easier to live each day like it's your last when you know it actually is."

If I'd known that my energy was limited to a finite quan-tity, perhaps I would have spent it more wisely. As it is, I'm learning to be more discerning with my time. And I've started to consider little things like sleep, healthy food, and an occa-sional pedicure now and again part of my jing-replenishing regime.

If you still have some jing, take my advice, don't waste it on longing for perfect jewelry, fighting over the toilet paper roll, or worrying about work. And if you're tapped out, like me, I'll see you in line for the wheatgrass smoothies.

6

Why Isn't Marriage as Exciting as Dating?

"Gravitation cannot be held responsible for two people falling in love."

—ALBERT EINSTEIN

Sex, Stress, and Cellulite: A Recipe for Love

"I'm too fat and tired to have sex."

If you haven't said it or thought it, chances you are, you've heard it—either from your wife or a group of women, lamenting their lack of libido.

Exhaustion and poor body image are often two big stumbling blocks for women when it comes to sex. Either we're too tired for a romp in the hay, or we're too weird about our bodies to enjoy it.

The flat-line-versus-frisky phenomenon has been mourned by husbands around the world and documented by women's magazines and talk shows from coast to coast. The most commonly cited cause is stress. Study after study has confirmed what every woman alive already knew: If your life makes you feel like the frayed end of a rope, you're hardly in the mood for love.

It's completely natural for a woman who feels overwhelmed to lose her sex drive. After all, Mother Nature gave us a sex drive so we would reproduce. If you can't handle the life you've got, the last thing nature wants is for you to produce another one. A woman's libido crashes and burns under stress—Mother Nature's instant birth control.

Men, however, often respond differently. The male brain makes the leap from, "I'm under stress," to, "I might not survive," to, "I better leave a little reminder of me in this world before I keel over," faster than you can say "testosterone surge."

There's a pretty simple solution to this problem, right? Reduce the stress and women will want to have more sex. (Hint to men: Simply telling your wife not to worry about the grocery shopping, childcare, cooking, cleaning, and driving will not reduce her stress. However, you actually taking over some of these jobs is pure erotica.)

But while stress may be a completely logical, natural, and even curable cause of low sex drive, I suspect that poor body image is an even more insidious problem. For some bizarre reason, we often believe that only the great-looking people get should have sex. Or, I should say, we women believe that. Very few men worry that their beer gut will interfere with an intimate encounter. But if a woman thinks she's fat, flabby, or anything less than a 10, she's often so fixated on her flaws that she can't enjoy the moment.

I personally blame television. Glamour girls and guys are seen gleefully tumbling around in bed every afternoon on the soaps, but when was the last time you saw an overweight, middle-aged, married couple hanging from the chandelier?

Sex expert Michael Alvear (MichaelAlvear.com) host of the British hit show, *Sex Inspectors*, says, "In all the people I've interviewed and worked with, I have not encountered a single woman who did not have some sense of body shame."

If every woman in England has something she doesn't like about her body, I'm guessing every woman in America does, too.

Alvear goes on to describe one woman on a recent show who was so uptight about her body that "she would only have sex when the lights were out. They were under the covers, and without getting too graphic, they were doing it in such a way that her husband could not see her body."

"My heart just sank," says Alvear. "Her husband thinks she has a beautiful body, but it was really painful to hear the depths of her shame."

As usual, the husband doesn't even notice—and may even love—the roll around his wife's middle, but the woman is all wigged out about it. The issue here isn't whether or not you have jiggle thighs. The problem is that we've been programmed to believe that a woman's biggest contribution in the bedroom is her body. She is an object to be presented, and if the presentation is not flawless, the sex will not be good. Alvear says, "The biggest problem for women in the bedroom is the mirror."

I have to wonder what would happen if women started thinking about themselves as active participants, the way men do. Instead of assuming that the way you look will determine the outcome, think about the way you feel, physically and emotionally, and the way you can make your partner feel.

It's always weird to talk about sex, and almost every time I write about it people send me letters accusing me of being a smut queen. But isn't it a little strange that we don't want to talk about a subject so many people are having problems with?

I'd hate to think of millions of stressed-out, flabby women out there suffering from low libido simply because nobody told them that chubby girls can have great sex.

So here's the bottom line: Sex is the great equalizer. Everybody's had it, including your mother. And everybody deserves to enjoy it, no matter what you look like or how behind you are on the laundry. Sex was meant to be one of the most fabulous emotional, physical, and, yes, spiritual joys of life, so don't let the size of your thighs or your to-do list ruin it for you.

Kleenex or Court Costs?

I'm going through the big *D*, and I don't mean Dallas. I'm talking about *divorce.*

No, it's not me—at least not this week—but my friends' marriages seem to be curdling faster than last year's eggnog. And as a bystander to the breakups, I can't help but feel incredibly sad.

Over the years I've watched couple after couple divvy up the fondue forks, the kids, the credit card debt, and arrange visitation schedules for the family ferret; and every time I think, "There, but for the grace of God and a few highly paid counselors, go I."

I've been married over twenty years. I spent the first ten trying to change my husband, the next five miserable that I couldn't, and only in the last five years have I finally gotten a clue as to what this game is all about.

It's kind of funny the way we romanticize marriage. The public failure rate is over fifty percent, and I suspect the private failure rate is closer ninety percent. Yet for some reason when the road gets rocky, we often blame the problems on ourselves—or, more often, on our spouses. We rarely stop to think that mastering marriage is more challenging than it is for a middle-aged man to do a back-handspring. The fact that you're failing doesn't mean you or your spouse are doing it wrong; it means it's hard.

Society tends to promote the fallacy that if we choose the right person, life will be bliss. It sounds good in theory, but when you're operating under the delusion that another person can and should make you happy, it's not too hard to understand why most people assume marital troubles mean you've made a bad match.

Several years ago, I was in the pre-fantasy of divorce myself. It's when you don't actually say the word out loud, but you spend a lot of time fantasizing about what life might be like without your spouse—who you should have married, who you might marry now if you had the chance, and how perfect your life might be if only your spouse wasn't around to mess it up.

During that time, I happened to read *The Unexpected Legacy of Divorce* by Judith Wallerstein. If you ever want a wake-up call about what a divorce can do to your kids, read it. (It's not pretty.)

Then, just as I was growing weary of the one-woman pity party, an invitation came to a marriage workshop based on Harville Hendrix's book, *Getting the Love You Want*. It opened the door for my husband and me to find happiness,

romance, and a real, grown-up love that is much more satisfying than the TV version I'd been longing for.

Oprah says Hendrix's Imago therapy model (Imago-
Therapy.com) radically changed her views on relationships
forever, and I agree. We got more out of that one weekend
than we did the previous thirty-seven rounds of traditional
he says/she says finger-pointing counseling.

Wallerstein's divorce book guilted me into hanging in
there, and two years later Hendrix's workshop changed the
direction of our entire lives. Today, we have a truly happy
marriage, something we both once thought was impossible—at least with each other.

Marriage is a tough gig, and I'm sure some people would
be better off divorced, but I don't believe that's true for more
than half of us. Every happily married, long-term couple I
know has struggled through serious issues. My husband and
I try to be very upfront about our past marital misery in
the hopes that it might break some of the silence and shame
associated with marriage problems and help other couples see
that it's almost never too far gone.

If your goal is to find true happiness, call a counselor
before you call a lawyer. The hourly rate is about the same,
but the lifetime payout makes it a much better investment.

The Truth About Weddings—For Better Or Worse

Some people just don't understand the importance of a perfect wedding. Whether it's the bridesmaid who refuses to
wear lavender or the cheapskate uncle who won't fly his entire
family across the country to attend, there's always somebody
who isn't with the program.

If you've ever planned a wedding or been in one, you know

how they often take on a life of their own. Forget the marriage—the ceremony and reception are what really count.

I once read a Dear Abby column in which—and I swear I am not making this up—a woman wrote in two months before her wedding to complain because her future sister-in-law had just announced that she was pregnant. This woman had been planning her wedding for more than a year, and now her sister-in-law was going to be five months along and showing when she walked down the aisle in her bridesmaid's dress.

Even worse, the poor bride-to-be suspected this was a planned pregnancy, that her selfish sister-in-law did it knowing this all-important wedding was coming up, and that the bridesmaid's dresses with the fitted waists would look terrible over a swollen belly!

The concluding questions for Abby were: Didn't she think the gestating sister-in-law was being horribly self-centered? And how should the bride go about telling her future in-law that, due to her thoughtless actions in getting pregnant, she was no longer invited to be in the wedding?

Good thing I don't answer letters like Abby does. I think I would have found out where the wedding was and showed up in the front pew with three squalling infants and a grubby toddler hopped up on Twinkies.

It's amazing how many people overestimate the importance of their own wedding in the lives of others.

A friend of mine told me that after he and his wife eloped, one of their friends quit speaking to them because they had the audacity to elope a mere two months before her wedding. The soon-to-be-married bride was aghast because the two couples shared many mutual friends, and now everybody at her wedding was going to be congratulating the newly eloped couple on their marriage. She just knew it would take all the attention from her, the bride with the real wedding.

Can you say "high maintenance?" Let's just hope she and the groom love each other to pieces because I don't see this pair holding on to many long-term friends.

It's easy to understand how weddings get out of control. After all, there's an entire industry devoted to making them perfect, and every time you open *People* magazine another celebrity is tying the knot by walking down a 257-foot aisle of hand-woven silk. I personally find it hilarious that celebrity weddings have become the Tiffany standard to which so many couples aspire. If ever a group of people had a horrible track record for marriage, it would be celebrities.

It's probably no coincidence that long-married celebs Paul Newman and Joanne Woodward's wedding photos reveal him in an everyday suit and her in a simple dress, cutting a small cake while an intimate group of friends looks on.

Yet we continue to believe that a perfect wedding equals a perfect life. And we let images of big-budget, superstar weddings cheapen what should be a deeply personal and meaningful event in our own lives—not a celebrity-for-a-day pageant.

I think one reason people go so crazy over weddings is because every vendor they speak with tries to convince them that their wedding day is the most important event of the year. "Your flowers will be fabulous, Darling, just like Trista and Ryan's." Or, "You look spectacular in that gown, kind of like Kevin Costner's new wife." It's pretty easy to lose perspective when an entire team of people is chanting, "It's your day! It's your day!" At that point, every decision seems monumental.

Steak or Chicken? Bubbles or birdseed? Cummerbunds or

vests? It doesn't matter if you're deciding whether to personalize the toothpicks or how many disposable cameras should be on each table, every decision feels like you'll doom your marriage if you make the wrong choice. And while you can eat with your elbows on the table your entire life, if you mess up the seating chart for the reception, you and your spouse are setting the stage for a life of bad manners.

People often view their weddings as the chance to start a new life with a clean slate, to become a more sophisticated, happier person with better barware and decent sheets.

You feel like your life will be changed on that one day, and the more perfect you can make it, the happier you'll be. The shocker is that life does change after you get married, but it doesn't have anything to do with matching towels and whether or not you served shrimp at the reception.

A beautiful wedding may cost thousands of dollars and take a team of people months to create. But creating a beautiful marriage requires even more work.

And the only people who can ruin that are you and your spouse.

Multi-Tasking Your Way to an Affair

Great news! Women have broken through another barrier on the road to achieving full parity with men. A *Newsweek* cover story reveals that women now cheat on their spouses almost as often as men.

Hurrah, hurrah! For every sleazy, bald guy "doing it" with his secretary, there is now a middle age woman peeling it off for the pool boy. And just when I thought the fight for equality was going to come up short, here we have conquered another exciting frontier.

Women have proven we can be just as indiscriminate with our bodies as men. The *Newsweek* article suggests that women are having more affairs because they're out and about meeting interesting people of the opposite sex, and they're no longer dependent on their spouses for economic support. The women who cheated said they loved the attention, the emotional connection, and the thrill of it.

My question is, where do they find the time? I barely have time to spend with my own husband, much less go out and pursue somebody else's. These women must have way more energy than I do. Turns out that while I'm wasting my time on the computer answering boring e-mails and mindlessly hunting for bargains on E-Bay, friskier women are surfing the net for men. Talk about multi-taskers. They can work, take care of the kids, answer the phone, and still have time for a nooner.

The *Newsweek* article also cited over-scheduled, stressed out lives as one of the main causes of female infidelity. Call me crazy, but wouldn't cheating on your spouse make your life even more of a challenge to manage? The brainpower and scheduling skills required to conduct and cover up an illicit affair would send my Palm Pilot into overload.

Another thing I wonder about is how do these women get over the weirdness of somebody new seeing you naked?

At least my husband knows I used to have a great body. Since his late night ice cream runs and the two very large children he impregnated me with are the primary causes of my jiggle belly, it's not so awful to let him see it. But I'd rather try on bathing suits under fluorescent lights than let some other guy see my purple stretch marks. Forget morality; sheer vanity is enough to make me keep my clothes on. All

I can say is, there must be large amounts of alcohol involved for cheaters over forty.

Therapists report that up to forty percent of their married female clients are cheating on their spouses. These aren't just a few bored, rich housewives messing around with their personal trainers. These are mainstream wives and mothers making some pretty life-altering decisions. Nobody knows what goes on inside somebody else's marriage, even the nicest guys can be terrible husbands. And loneliness is a powerful, awful feeling, no matter how nice your surroundings.

But haven't women learned from the mistakes of men? Affairs are always more trouble than they're worth. And when the thrill of the new wears off, you're usually just left with a slightly better-looking version of what you were bored with in the first place.

You would think, as the more creative sex, women would have enough imagination to save themselves the trouble. If you can compose the grocery list in your head while you're doing it, you ought to be able to conjure up a mental image of Brad Pitt any time you need him. And if you want variety, most of the husbands I know would gladly dress up as a fireman or construction worker to spice up the action.

Ironically enough, most of the wives who cheated said what they really wanted was more love and attention. And given first choice, they said they would have preferred getting it from their husbands rather than potentially reeking havoc on their lives with an affair. If love and attention are what women want, perhaps we need to expand our definitions. A guy who goes to work, cuts the grass, and gives the kids a bath may not seem like a Romeo. But if he's doing his best just to get by, maybe his ego needs a boost as much as yours does.

Keeping together a long-term marriage isn't as fun or exciting as the flattering attention of someone new. But this is one arena where women don't need to make more inroads.

If you're a man reading this, you're probably relieved to hear somebody suggest that women need to go easy on the expectations. But before you pick up the remote, let me share with you this universal truth: Romancing a woman is not a one-time event. Disregard this information, and the person you cheat the most is yourself.

Spontaneous flowers, sappy words on a card written by a gay guy in a cubicle at Hallmark, and a babysitter she didn't have to arrange for will get you more brownie points with your wife than a $150 dinner did while you were dating.

A woman who feels loved is a beautiful thing to see. And a man who's smart enough to put forth a little effort gets to look at one every day.

"You Complete Me," and Other Lies I Believed About Love

"You complete me."

When Tom Cruise uttered those memorable words to Renee Zellweger in *Jerry Maguire*, he summed up all the romantic hopes and dreams so many of us have for love. We want a soul mate—that perfect romantic partner who completes us, that wondrous person who understands our minds, whose mere presence makes us feel happy and whole.

But how many of us get romance right in round one of marriage? The divorce rate is over fifty percent, and many other couples remain physically married but lead emotionally separate lives.

I can count on one hand the number of couples I know

who have created truly happy partnerships and sustained them over the long haul.

When people talk about soul mates, usually they're in the beginning of a relationship or at the end of one. They're either waxing on all doe-eyed and simpering about how they've found their one true love, a person they have yet to share a checkbook or bathroom with, but with whom they know eternal bliss will be found. Or they're sadly realizing their current partner is not who they really want and secretly are fantasizing about the one they let get away.

But do soul mates even exist? Is there such thing as one human being who can make us whole? Soul mate is, by its very definition, a spiritual concept. My favorite marriage expert, Dr. Harville Hendrix, has cracked the code on the soul mate debate and unlocked the secret of lasting love.

He says we unconsciously choose a partner who will push our buttons in order for us to grow. We're attracted to "someone who has both the positive and negative traits of our parents." That's why we feel so wonderfully at home in the beginning, then find our partner so horribly annoying as the relationship matures.

Hendrix suggests your life's work as a couple is to replay your childhood stuff over and over again, until both of you learn a different response. Early infatuation and later disillusionment are all part of the master plan. Mother Nature, God, the Tooth Fairy, or whomever you believe in wants your soul to grow. But the powers that be also know that you're too smart to fall for someone who opens the dating dialogue with, "Hook up with me, I'll notice all your flaws, bring out all your childhood issues, and try like heck to overhaul your entire personality." Instead, the universe sends you a hot honey who, at first glance, promises to make all your romantic dreams come true. But when the glow fades and the toilet seat wars begin, our first inclination is to cast our mate aside leaving a pile of discarded lovers, unpaid lawyer bills, and leftover children in our wake.

Yet many people trade in their partner for whatever romance lies behind door number three—usually someone with exactly the same inner workings as the person they left behind. Different packaging on the outside but the same emotional map within. I have to believe life would be easier, cheaper, and happier if we could make it work in round one.

At the core of Hendrix's work is the idea that what your partner needs the most from you is exactly the area where you need to grow. Read that sentence twice, because if you can embrace that concept, you will dramatically change your relationship forever.

And it literally can happen overnight

Whether it's more words of affirmation, accepting them the way they are, or even just learning to show up on time, whatever your partner keeps nagging you to do, just do it. The harder it is for you, the more you probably need to do it.

The great thing about this philosophy is that it means your partner really does need to change in exactly the way you think they should. The downside is—the same thing applies to you. We're given a gift as human beings: a soul mate, a person ideally suited to push our buttons, and someone needing more than we think we should have to give. Throw one away, and the universe almost always sends you another one.

The truth is, you don't find a soul mate. With your partner's help, you complete yourself and become one. Learn to play your part right, and you'll discover real love, something much more romantic than anything Hollywood could create.

7

Does the Buddha Need Botox?

*"I'm a Barbie girl in a Barbie world.
Life in plastic, it's fantastic."*

—BARBIE GIRL (RADIO)

Fading Reflections of a Has-Been Hottie

Mirror, mirror, on the wall, who's aging faster than them all?

Losing your looks can be hard. One minute you're pretty hot, the next minute you're just plain pretty, and before you know it, you're a mature woman whom construction workers ask for directions.

The transition from Miss to Ma'am is often tough, especially if you fancied yourself a hottie back in the day. I look at pictures of myself in my late teens and twenties and wonder why I didn't spend every waking moment in a bikini.

As it was, I spent my college years in dirty sweats and my twenties in boxy, man-like suits, trying to look mature enough—and sexless enough—to feel qualified for my job. By the time I had enough confidence to strut my stuff, my stuff wasn't strut-able material, at least not during daytime hours.

We women look back at our younger selves and wonder

why we ever thought we weren't good enough. And we look at our aging selves and wonder when time is going to stop playing such cruel tricks on us.

I know there are many women who may have never felt pretty, and maybe to them aging comes more gracefully. But as egotistical as this sounds, there was a brief period in my life when I knew I was drop-dead good-looking, and quite frankly, I miss it. I never thought I was so shallow as to be dependent on my looks. But when you're used to making heads turn, it's kind of hard when it goes away. Looking at my mug shot or a full body shot of me on my web site (Forget-Perfect.com) you can see that I'm still a reasonably attractive forty-ish woman, but unless I start cruising the halls of a nursing home, the days when I could make armies of men drool are long gone.

Who would have thought a happily married mother of two would care so much about male attention? But a quick survey of my friends reveals that I'm not the only one who finds it depressing when a room full of men look right through you as though you don't exist.

Still, as hard as it is to lose your looks in the privacy of the suburbs, I can't imagine how awful it would be to watch yourself age on the silver screen. At least as a writer, when I get old and fat, I can keep my job. However, a quick glance at Meg Ryan's bizarrely puffed lips demonstrates that all the money and plastic surgeons in the world can't keep you looking twenty-five forever.

The few celebs sliding into older ages with their dignity intact are just like the regular women doing the same thing. They're the ones who are happy enough with their insides for their outsides to reflect some of the glow. Susan Sarandon, the poster child for sexy middle age, isn't reed thin, and although it's been rumored that she's gone under the knife, her eyes can still move around in her head and even blink.

I actually went to high school with Sandra Bullock, and although I wouldn't want to stand next to her in a leotard like I did for our gymnastics picture, I'm relieved to see that the former giggly goofball in fifth-period drama class still looks pretty much like herself. Sandy may be a better-toned, better-dressed, thinner forty-something than I am, but she's not trying to pretend she's twenty.

As a non-movie star mom, I know that one day I'll look back on the way I look right now and think I was magnificent. So I guess if the reflection I see in others' eyes doesn't mirror that image, I'll just have to start seeing it for myself.

Where Have All the Dumb Girls Gone?

Remember when being pretty was associated with not being very smart? Beautiful and blond meant ditzy and dumb, and the studious girls were Plain Janes, whose glasses and frumpy wardrobes advertised their high IQs.

A quick glance at the contestants on the TV show, *The Apprentice*, makes it clear that sexy is no longer synonymous with stupid. When all the young hopefuls line up to meet Trump, it looks more like a casting call for a toothpaste commercial than it does a business meeting.

With TV being a visual medium, reality shows search for genetically superior specimens, but the fact that there are so many razor-smart people who look like bathing suit models tells me things have changed.

Have we improved the gene pool? Were the dumb jocks

and their airhead girlfriends so busy gazing into the mirror they forgot to reproduce? Or did all the smart people suddenly discover teeth bleaching kits and eyebrow waxing?

Perhaps there were always lots of hot, intelligent women out there, and after years of watching their mothers play dumb, the current generation of daughters has decided the jig is up.

I suspect it's all of the above.

For centuries, beauty has been a woman's most valuable currency. Driven by an evolutionary desire to produce healthy offspring, men sought out mates who were good-looking. A woman's sparkly teeth, shiny hair, and desirable waist-to-hip ratio meant she had good genes and was hardy enough to pop out a few bambinos, who could carry on the family name.

Women on the other hand, traditionally looked for good providers—men who were intelligent enough to bag the big buffalo and collect the resources needed to ensure the survival of the kids.

So an attractive woman marries an intelligent man, and the cream rises. Mother Nature combines the best genes of both parents, and eventually you wind up with an Aphrodite MBA. But if natural selection has been going on since the dawn of time, what's with the seemingly recent surge in overachieving hotties, particularly those of the female variety? Each generation may move up a rung or two on the evolutionary ladder, with people slowly getting smarter and better looking over time. But what's really morphed the process forward in the last few decades is not changes in our gene pool, but changes in our attitudes toward brains and beauty.

Images of women like Helen Gurley Brown, who showed

us sexy women could have careers, and Katherine Hepburn, who wore pants and played characters as smart as she was, opened the door for women's brains to come out of the lingerie drawer. The "smarts are okay" tipping point came when legions of divorced women had to go out and earn a living in the 1970s and discovered that they—just like Mary Tyler Moore—could look good and be competent at the same time. And when the first crew of female MBAs decided to shuck their mini-man pinstripe suits and red bowties in favor of sandals and clingy knits, all bets were off. Sexy and smart was here to stay.

Years ago Jane Mansfield was a brainy brunette who couldn't get a part, but once she dyed her hair blond and dropped her IQ 30 points, suddenly she was Hollywood's *it* girl. While Tinseltown may still be decorated with its fair share of dumb-bunny starlets, smart women no longer have to dumb themselves down to get ahead—in the movie industry or in the real world.

The good news: For every woman who ever felt like she had to pull her hair back in a bun and don knee-length skirts with dowdy shoes in order to be taken seriously in board meetings, the days of stifling your femininity are over.

The bad news: Now that the smart-and-sexy combo is okay, it's becoming the cultural norm. Knockout presentations aren't enough, anymore. If you really want to be successful, your PowerPoint had better be accompanied by cleavage and stiletto heels.

My father, a retired executive who has interviewed and managed hundreds of young men and women, says, "Smart, good-looking people always do better in life." It's a fact I find both accurate and depressing. I've gone through a cute phase, and now I like to believe I'm in a smart one. But trying to combine them both as I move through my forties feels like more work than I'm willing to do.

However, just as we've redefined "smart," perhaps its time to redefine "sexy" as well. If being dumb no longer is considered attractive, who's to say that flat stomachs aren't overrated as well?

The day of the dumb girl may be gone forever; let's just hope the day of the wise and wrinkled is soon to come.

Is Fat the New Thin?

They say you can never be too rich or too thin, but everybody knows you certainly can be too poor or too fat.

But now there's great news for all of us whose thighs rub together when we walk:

Excess body fat is no longer limited to the poor. The rich are now saddled with the same affliction as the burger-lovin', french fry-eatin' masses. Recent studies reveal that while the poor continue to gain weight, the rich are now the fastest-growing segment of the obese population.

Apparently, it doesn't matter whether you're overindulging in foie gras or chicken nuggets, it all looks the same when it hits your hips. But the big question is: Will cellulite have the same negative stigma now that it's hanging around (and off) rich people?

A recent study from Rice University has found that many folks, especially retailers, haven't yet wised up to the idea that porkie people have wallets just as big as their backsides.

Psychology grad students Jennessa Shapiro and Eden King dressed up in "fat suits" to see what kind of response they would get from store personnel. They, along with eight other students, proved what anyone carrying around a few extra pounds already knows: Fat people get worse service just about everywhere but Jenny Craig. The sales clerks spent less time with the two students, and in several instances store employees were downright rude. It was a night-and-day difference from the way they were treated when they entered the stores as their normal, thin selves. The only exception was when the women walked in wearing the rubber blubber suits, carrying a diet soda, and talking about losing weight, then the sales clerks actually treated them with respect.

Shapiro, a slim twenty-five-year-old blond, says, "I was blown away by the experience. Obesity instantly gets you second-class treatment."

I shudder to think how the clerks would have reacted if instead of just pretending to be fat, the students had also been made up to look unattractive and old as well. Rather than just ignoring them, the entire sales force probably would have formed a human barricade and refused to let them come into the mall at all.

Perception is everything. Centuries ago extra girth was associated with status and wealth. Perhaps if the sales clerks in the Rice University study had lived in the Middle Ages, they would have welcomed the portly women with open arms. They would have known their weight was a clear sign that these women could afford the latest in fur capes to keep them comfy in the castle. But somewhere along the line things changed. Rich women discovered cigarettes and amphetamines, and suddenly, thin was in.

As someone who has been both heavy and thin at various points in her life, I can you tell you firsthand that people make all kinds of assumptions about you when you're overweight.

I unwittingly conducted my own one-woman sociological study on the fat vs. thin phenomenon a few years back. Six months after the birth of my second child I did a nationwide seminar series when I was forty pounds overweight. And I noticed a distinct difference in audience response to a plus-sized speaker.

It took a while for me to figure out what was going on, but after a few groups I realized that when the old me—the cute, thin one—walked on stage, crowds were eager to hear what I had to say. But when Miz Plump came out, it took longer to get the audience engaged.

Ironically enough, my fat vs. thin experience happened at a time when my confidence was at an all-time high. I had emerged victorious from a two-year saga that included a late-pregnancy miscarriage, followed by an anxious nine-month gestation, and an extremely painful, "Sorry, honey, the baby is coming too fast for the good drugs" birth.

I'd finally had a healthy baby, and quite frankly, after what I'd been through, I thought I looked great. To me, my extra rolls of flab were the meaningless byproducts of a job well done. A highly fashionable, size fourteen friend had loaned me half a closet of designer duds, so I went on stage feeling fine. Imagine my surprise when I found myself having to dig my way out of the "She's fat, so she must be stupid and lazy, too" hole right from the start.

I might not have been giving off a "no-confidence, loser" vibe to begin with, but it sure was hard not to sink into one based on the reaction I got from others. But with more and more people sharing the same problem, perhaps fat is going to become the great equalizer. And if the rich keep piling on the pounds, who knows? Maybe fat will become the new thin, and before you know it, we'll all be rolling in the dough.

Nobody Feels Beautiful While She's Getting a Boob Job

"Don't hate me because I'm beautiful."

Don't worry, honey, the other ninety-eight percent of us non-beautiful people are too busy obsessing about our own flaws to put much emotional energy toward thinking about you.

According to a recent study, only two percent of women describe themselves as beautiful. My first thought was, two percent, how pathetic is that? Thousands of women from around the globe were asked, and only two percent think they're beautiful? But then I polled a few of my friends, and I couldn't find a single one who said she was beautiful. Now, I'm wondering where they even came up with the two percent. Have we all gone insane?

The multi-national study, "The Real Truth about Beauty: A Global Report," reveals what we always suspected—none of us are happy with the way we look. But the part I found most fascinating was that while only two percent of women say they are beautiful, sixty-two percent of American women say they feel beautiful when they're doing something spiritual.

This seems like a pretty simple problem. If doing something spiritual makes us feel beautiful, why aren't we doing more of it?

Nobody says she feels beautiful while she's getting collagen shot into her lips or bags of silicon shoved into her chest, and I also suspect most of the women starving themselves don't feel too attractive either.

The key difference here is when asked if we are beautiful, we think about the outside, but when asked what makes us feel beautiful, we think about the inside. It's the difference between how we look and how we feel. As much as we may think the answer to our beauty woes is a new lip liner, this truly is a spiritual problem. We can continue to keep whacking away at the outside of our bodies or we can take a deeper look within.

I can only imagine what my mother, who died of breast cancer more than ten years ago, would have thought had she seen the line of empty-hearted women waiting to have their chests and faces cut open in the hopes of becoming "The Swan." We may say we feel beautiful when we're spiritual, but I have yet to see a reality show where female contestants are judged based on who can light a better menorah or who can hold the longest bow toward Mecca.

But there is hope. Dove, the company which is owned by Unilever, is the sponsor of "The Real Truth about Beauty" study. Having been employed by a mongo, corporate conglomerate once myself, I am typically loathe to give one any kudos. My general perception of big beauty companies is that they make their money by convincing us that we all look and smell so bad we shouldn't leave the house without dousing ourselves in their products.

However, in this case I was pleasantly surprised to discover that Dove commissioned Dr. Nancy Etcoff, a Harvard professor, and Dr. Susie Orbach from the London School of Economics to investigate "our society's narrow definition of beauty and the implications it has on women."

And I have to tell you, I love what they have done with the results. Their new ad campaigns feature women of every size and skin and their web site—CampaignforRealBeauty. com—includes a dazzling photo of a ninety-five-year-old woman.

She's not some pasty-face grandma stooped over in a rocking chair with her eyes down. She's olive skinned; she's laughing; she's looking right into the camera; and she's more alive than any of the tight-faced, expressionless, Botoxed women you see at the country club. In a word, she's beautiful. And she knows it. It may have taken her close to a hundred years to get there, but she's among the two percent.

For the first time in my life, I actually hope a big company sells more stuff as a result of its ad campaign. It will prove women know what real beauty is, and we respond to it when we see it.

That ninety-five-year-old woman isn't the "before" shot or a warning photo about reducing the signs of aging. She *is* the good-looking one. She's the kind of woman we can all aspire to be, a woman who looks her age and glows from the inside out.

If you've got any doubt that inner spirituality is the secret of real beauty, I challenge you to look into the eyes of somebody who truly glows. It will tell you everything you need to know.

Next time you're having a bad hair day, don't hate yourself because you're not beautiful. Stand in front of the mirror, look yourself right in the eye, sing "Amazing Grace," and remind yourself why you are.

Two percent. Ladies...we've got some work to do.

8

What if Peace was Sexy?

*"Foreign policy today, irrespective of what we might wish,
in its impact on our daily lives, overshadows everything else.
Expenditures, taxation, domestic prosperity,
the extent of social services—
all hinge on the basic issue of war or peace."*

—CONGRESSMAN JACK KENNEDY, 1951

First Class Baby from Dayton

His name is Adam. I met him on a flight from Dayton to
Atlanta. I was going home; he was going back to Iraq.

He had a coach ticket, but the flight attendant bumped
him up to business class. It was a nice gesture, but I'm guessing that a free drink and a little extra leg room didn't mean
much to the buzz-cut, young man in brown desert fatigues.
As he stowed his duffel in the overhead bin and slid into the
seat next to me, the man across the aisle gave him a respect-
ful nod.

He was going back, he said. He'd been home for two weeks
on leave, and now it was time to return. He was a machine
gunner. His sister was in the Army, too, and his parents were
watching her two-year-old child while she was overseas.

"I'm glad I got to come home," he said. "It reminds me what I'm fighting for."

"What's it like over there?" I asked.

"It sucks," he said.

"Was it hard to be home?"

"Yeah, it was. Excuse my language, ma'am, but y'all bitch about nothin'. Like, oh, I ran into a pothole. Over there, the whole road's a pothole. I used to be like all the rest of you, but I'm different now."

His job was to ride in a turret at the top of a tank and "clear things out." I didn't understand the technical terms, so it took me a few minutes to realize he was scouring the roads for enemies, not clearing out brush.

"Sometimes you can't tell," he said. "You show 'em your weapon, you try to throw a water bottle or somethin' at them, you fire a warning shot, but if they keep comin' at you, you have to take care of it."

He had to shoot someone recently, a sniper trying to take out his driver.

He said: "Sometimes, you just have to say it—killin' people's not easy. In the moment, you don't think about it, but afterwards you do.

"Lots of times there are kids running around. Sometimes I give them money, but mostly they just get in your way."

At one point, he seemed so jittery, I thought he might jump out of his skin. When he talked about killing, behind his eyes, I felt the sickening, clammy presence of a frantic little boy's soul screaming to get out. He had what soldiers call the "thousand-yard stare." A glazed look that implies, "My body may be here, but, mentally, I'm somewhere else."

He didn't like to reveal his emotions, he said. "It's like

playing poker every day. They don't know what you got, and you don't know what they got. This is all they get," he said, as he set his jaw, tightened his lips and hardened his brow.

I guess I'm getting older, because I didn't see a seasoned combat veteran. I saw a nice, young kid from Dayton who might be dead within a week.

"Does your mother know how dangerous it is?" I asked.

"Hell, no. I lie to my mamma," he said with a laugh. "All the smart guys do; you don't want nobody worrying about you like that." He'd also gotten a "Dear John" call while he was in Iraq. "But I didn't show nothin,'" he said.

As we left the plane, I asked if he needed directions.

"I'll just find the USO, but first I need to grab a smoke."

As he headed into the glass enclosure, I wanted to give him a hug. I wanted to tell him I would be thinking about him. I wanted to tell him I was sorry we couldn't come up with a better solution to our problems.

But how do you tell a twenty-three-year-old soldier that you think he's somebody's baby? "Good luck, son," I choked, as I laid my hand on his arm.

I sobbed the whole way home.

Strong Words from the Mouth of a Babe
Your kids are watching you, and they're observing the rest of the universe as well. The stunning clarity with which they can assess things often amazes me.

My daughter recently wrote an essay for a book entitled *If Women Ruled the World*.

Imagine my shock when my then eleven-year-old, who previously specialized in fantasy tales about magical cats, produced a piece that summed up the lunacy of war in two short paragraphs. She wrote it in about an hour, with absolutely no help at all from her mother. I returned home from a lecture trip last spring and found it lying on my desk.

Political leaders can yammer on all they like about how complicated things are, but I think she hits the nail on the head:

"Our Best Creations Would Last Beyond Age 18"
By Elizabeth McLeod, age 11

I believe if women ruled the world, we would all learn from an early age that the job of every human being is to improve the Earth. There would not be wars and bombings of innocent people. Women know what it means when the news says, "Two people were killed in Iraq." They can imagine how the mother felt to have her miracle destroyed. That is what war is, when you think about it: destruction of the millions of miracles women have made.

It takes about 8.25 years of a woman's actual physical labor to raise an 18-year-old person. A child takes 100 percent of the mother's time the first two years, 50 percent of her time the next six years, and about 25 percent of her time from ages 9 to 18, for a total of 8.25 years of labor. Multiply 8.25 by the thousands killed in war and you have billions of years of actual woman's labor put to waste in one war. You see, women get that number and shake their heads in disgust. They know the value of those years and the pain of the next 50 years, living with a broken heart.

I couldn't even fathom where she got the idea until I remembered our recent trip to France. Besides doing the tourist gawk at the Eiffel Tower, the Louvre, and all the other beautiful things first-timers see in Paris, we also visited memorials to World Wars I and II.

As we watched the grainy footage of Adolf Hitler and his goose-stepping troops, she commented on how young all the boys looked. When we learned that a quarter of all French men between eighteen and thirty—about 1.3 million of them—were killed in World War I, I was embarrassed that I couldn't even accurately describe the cause of it.

Later in Holland, as we stood in the Anne Frank house, we marveled at the power of a writer when we realized that more people had read Anne Frank's words than had read Hitler's. We discussed why strong, angry voices appeal to fear and bring out the worst in people, yet small, truthful expressions can touch humans at their core. As we talked about how great writers can shape our perspective on history, I didn't quite realize I was speaking with one at the time.

It took a kid to point out that the emperor had no clothes on. Maybe it's going to take a few kids to point out what we adults know, but are too afraid to say out loud: War is nothing but one mother's child killing another one. You can put as patriotic a face on it as you like, but when *People* magazine runs a list of 831 dead human beings in their Best and Worst issue, the secret is out.

We've been killing each other since the dawn of time, and it's not working any better now than it did then. I used to pray for peace, but now I'm praying for some great minds to come up with better ways to solve our problems.

I wish we could reach into the heart of every mother's child and create a different vision for our future.

My dream for my own child is that, eighty years from now, as she sits old and gray on her front porch, her granddaughter approaches and asks, "Grandma, did people really used to kill each other?"

And my daughter will describe, in her shaky and wavering voice, the thing they used to call "war." She will say, "People used to organize big groups for the sole purpose of attacking each other. They thought it was the only way to protect their values. But we're smarter now, so we don't do that anymore."

The world's children are watching us, and they're internalizing a core set of beliefs that will be very difficult for them to change when they grow up. Anne Frank said, "In spite of everything, I still believe that people are really good at heart." I am both humbled and amazed by her words and the words my own child has written. I am awed to think that I may be raising a future world leader, but then I quietly realize—we all are.

Peace on Earth to every mother's child. May you do goodwill with your mother's most amazing creation.

It's Kumbaya Week at West Point

There's nothing like a man in uniform to make a woman swoon. If Richard Gere strutted into my office in his dress whites, I'd throw my laptop out the window, jump into his arms, and hope he was more officer than gentleman.

But is putting on a uniform and being prepared to die for your country what it really means to be a man?

I come from a line of proud military men. My grandfather was buried with a twenty-one-gun salute in Arlington

National Cemetery, my father served on a Navy aircraft carrier, and my brother is a former Army Ranger.

As much as I admire our military, I have to wonder why we don't have a similar national structure devoted to peace. Prestigious academies teach the art of war to the finest minds we've got, but aside from the mommy mantra "hands aren't for hitting," who's out there teaching people how to create peace?

In 1792, a novel idea was introduced: to create a Department of Peace to "balance" the Department of War. Some of this nation's most esteemed leaders, including Thomas Jefferson and George Washington, supported it. Yet 223 years later we still don't have one.

To some people, "Secretary of Peace" brings to mind the image of a chanting swami in flowing white robes carrying a flock of trained doves. And a Peace Academy sounds more like a flower child retreat where the graduation ceremony includes three rounds of "Kumbaya" than it does a leader-grooming institution rivaling the prestige of West Point.

No one argues the need for a strong defense. But much like a savvy CEO counts on the differing perspectives of finance, operations, and sales to make good decisions, a growing movement is afoot to make sure the peace perspective has a seat at the table.

Congress is now considering a bill to create a U.S. Department of Peace, headed by a Secretary of Peace who would be a member of the president's Cabinet. The bill (ThePeaceAlliance.com) also provides for a Peace Academy, a sister institution to our military academies where America's best and brightest would be trained in the cutting edge techniques of non-violent conflict resolution.

Is it the answer to all our problems? No, but it's a good start.

Peace is inevitable—and we can either begin the process now or we can wait until half the planet is dead. Generations of men and women didn't give their lives for us to keep repeating the same deadly scenarios over and over again. Walking under swords held by chiseled men ready to fight for your honor is a compelling vision, but another scenario makes me feel even more patriotic. It's graduation day at the Peace Academy. My daughter stands in her dress-white suit, her long blond hair pulled back in a bun. As she squares her shoulders and walks up to the platform, the military men of her family look on, some in spirit, some seated in the front row.

Her great-grandfather watches in his stiff green uniform, his hard-won colonel's eagles perched on his lapels. Her grandfather, the second-class petty officer with grease under his nails, who was arming nuclear bombs at age twenty-one, joins him, as does her uncle, an Army Ranger trained to survive torture and kill a man with his bare hands. As the pristine young woman walks under a canopy of flags and accepts her diploma, the three soldiers' eyes fill with tears. And as she turns to face the crowd, they rise. In unison they bring their hands to their brows to offer her a crisp salute. She is a leader. She is a patriot. She has made them proud.

Last fall my dad, former Petty Officer Jay Earle, spent three days straining his seventy-year-old arthritic knee to walk the halls of Congress with me talking to leaders about creating a U.S. Department of Peace.

An honorable man fights for his women. And a smart man knows that the best weapon isn't always a gun.

The Hero Conspiracy Against Men

We women have entered into an unspoken, but very well known and completely dysfunctional conspiracy with our men. We want them to be big strong heroes, yet we criticize them when they resort to violence.

We're mortified if our husband punches out a guy in a restaurant. But if the same man shoots down a bunch of enemy planes, he gets his own parade.

I'm proud of the service my family's men and so many others have provided for our country. But it's begun to dawn on me that we're putting these guys in a bit of a double bind.

If you know anything about men, you know that despite their sometimes baffling ways, in their hearts they truly want to please the women they love. In fact, the desire to please and protect women drives much of male behavior. But we women have somehow given them the mistaken idea that we're impressed when they kill each other.

In the distant past, it may have been absolutely necessary to have a guy who could protect you against a big bear. But if you think you're going safer living in a world where men continually apply their talents to perfecting the art of war, ask the women in Iraq how safe they're feeling these days.

I know there's evil in the world, and I would never argue against the need for a strong defense, but it's time we women gave our men the chance to be real heroes for generations to come.

Peace has been a human aspiration since the dawn of time. Yet when you talk about peace, some people assume you're anti-military or even anti-American. However, I see it as just the opposite. A country that wants peace needs to support our leaders in creating it. Many people have criticized the current and other presidents for starting wars. But have we ever really ever provided any of our presidents with the proper resources for creating peace?

After watching even more soldiers and civilians die, conservatives and liberals alike are finally beginning to agree that the Department of Peace is a good idea.

Beyond the obvious moral reasons—most of the big religions have pretty clear directives against killing each other—there are also some sound economic incentives. Planes and tanks cost big money, and losing your best and brightest on the battlefield is hardly an efficient use of national resources.

Just as taking care of your health is cheaper than surgery and education is cheaper than prison, proactively pursuing peace is preventative maintenance. It's a fiscally prudent solution that could save us a pile of dough.

But for me, the most compelling reason for a Department of Peace is personal—I'm tired of watching smart men die. If I see one more face of one more mother's child whose precious soul was murdered during the atrocities of battle, I think I'll throw up.

I don't claim to understand the inner workings of government bureaucracy, and I'm not sure how the logistics of the Department of Peace will eventually play out. But I do know that there's one thing every woman in America could do right now that would change the course of history forever. We could decide that peace was sexy.

We could let our men know that as much as we appreciate and honor the sacrifices they've made, we love them too much to watch them keep killing each other.

We women have more power than we know.

Men want to be the heroes, but we're the ones who write the job description.

9

How Much Guilt Can You Fit into a Briefcase?

"If It's Not One Thing,
It's Your Mother."

—ANITA RENFROE (BOOK TITLE)

Faux Housewives Found Guilty as Charged

"God, I can't believe how much guilt is in this room."

A judge barking at a line-up of third-strike DUI offenders? No, it was Erma Bombeck's son addressing a group of humor writers.

You'd think people who are paid to be funny would take life a little less seriously, but guilt was the mood of the day at the Erma Bombeck Humor Writers conference. Or at least, it was a constant theme for the women in the crowd.

The big angst among the mommy writers was the worry that every time they choose their keyboard over their kids, they were creating psycho killers. When the three grown Bombeck children took the stage for questions, instead of pumping them for information about where Erma got her ideas, how she got an eleven-year gig on *Good Morning*

America, or how a housewife from Dayton, Ohio, got her column syndicated into more than nine hundred papers, all the moms wanted to know was, "How did you all feel about your mother's work?"

Of course, what they really wanted to ask but were too polite to say was, "Are you three normal, or did she leave you by yourself all the time, and now you're a porn star?" For the record, the Bombeck "kids" are all functioning adults who seem about as close to normal as the rest of us. I'm friends with Betsy Bombeck, and her brothers, Andy and Matt, are just delightful as well.

But they are all amazed at how wracked with guilt the next generation of Erma wannabe's is over spending even a moment away from their kids. "Our mother went out on book tours for weeks at a time," says Betsy. Am I the only one who finds it rather ironic that America's favorite "housewife" was actually a multi-media mega-star? Yes, she had a home office, but she wasn't available to her children 24/7.

Mothers have worked since the dawn of time, whether it was bringing in the harvest or helping Pa Kettle keep the wolves at bay. The fabulous 1950's child-centered model of domesticity that many of us consider the norm was actually a bizarre blip in the history of motherhood. And truth be told, most of those Cleaver moms weren't down on the floor playing tea party or Legos all afternoon.

I often wonder if many working moms feel guilty because they've never spent endless hours at home. When you work full time, you picture the stay-at-home life as a nonstop bonding experience with your offspring. Lazy afternoons in the park, modeling clay at the kitchen table, and reading thirty-seven stories a day. But as someone who went from the fast track to the potty lane, I can promise you this: There's not as much cuddle time as you think.

Erma Bombeck wrote about housewives, but by the time people were reading her, she wasn't one. She gave a voice to legions of disgruntled women who didn't have one, but the main reason her writing was funny was because she enjoyed doing it.

The notion of getting joy from your work isn't a model we often see portrayed. These days the standard thinking is, if you work for groceries, you're a saint. But if your six-figure income is paying for a second home, you're selfish.

As a faux housewife myself—a woman who spends a lot of time in her home, but does no housework whatsoever, and is usually locked in her office while her children try to reach her via video conference from two floors below—I certainly experience my share of maternal remorse.

But one of my favorite Erma quotes is, "When I stand before God at the end of my life, I would hope that I would not have a single bit of talent left and could say, 'I used everything You gave me.'"

And I'm not going to feel guilty when I use it on something other than my kids.

Your Inner Ten-Year-Old: Career Coach to the Stars

What did you want to be when you were ten years old? Chances are you had a better handle on your own skills and talents than any guidance counselor you've met since then.

That's because when you're ten, the world hasn't started messing with you yet. You know exactly who you are because it never dawns on you that you're supposed to be anything different.

Dr. JoAnn Deak, the author of *Girls Will Be Girls*, says, "After surveying hundreds of females, it seems that female self-esteem declines soon after age ten and does not come back up out of that trough for many women until their 40s."

Three decades of low self-confidence? Good grief. Who knew, "I am woman," really meant, "Please pass the Prozac?"

I don't know if men go through the same thing—my husband tells me fifty was the turning point for him. But I know tons of women, including yours truly, who, at forty, finally feel comfortable in their own skin, however saggy it may be. It's almost like it takes you thirty years to get back to who you really are.

So why the three-decade detour?

It would be easy to blame it on men, marriage, and motherhood. But for every woman who lost her sense of self as she created her family, there are just as many others whose relationships unlocked what they had inside.

Contrary to popular belief, I don't think the problem is giving too much of yourself to others. It's trying to turn yourself into somebody you're not. Once we get the message that there's a right and a wrong way to be, we waste a good chunk of our lives trying to master the system.

Dr. Deak opens *Girls Will Be Girls* with a telling quote from twelfth-grader Nora:

"It's pretty hard being a girl nowadays. You can't be too smart, too dumb, too pretty, too ugly, too friendly, too coy, too aggressive, too defenseless, too individual, or too programmed. If you're too much of anything, then the others envy you, or despise you because you intimidate them or make them jealous. It's like you have to be everything and nothing all at once, without knowing which you need more of."

How many grown women have felt the same way?

We often spend our teens, twenties, and thirties trying to conform to whatever life model we think is the correct one. But by the time we're forty we've about had it with trying to live up to everybody else's expectations.

At ten and forty, women actually have a lot in common: We don't spend a lot of time worrying about what other people think. It's not that we don't care about others, but obsessing about their opinions seems as ridiculous as passing up free cake at a birthday party.

People talk about reinventing yourself at mid-life, but perhaps it's not so much a new invention as it is a discovery of what was there all along.

When you think about the dream you had for yourself when you were ten, what was it you really wanted? It doesn't matter what kind of career you did or didn't choose, the essence of who you really are can be found in your fourth- and fifth-grade dreams.

Whether you envisioned yourself as a rock star or a rodeo queen, a preacher or a teacher, there was some aspect of that job that appealed to you. The part of you that knew who you really are and what you're meant to do.

You can try to cover it up all you like and talk about how impractical it is, but you had a spark inside you back then, and stifling it is only going to make you miserable. The quicker you can find a way to ignite it, the happier you'll be.

I should know. When I was ten, I wanted to be the first kid editor of *Mad Magazine.* I carelessly abandoned the idea after a teacher bored me to death yammering on about how real editors are experts in spelling and grammar.

Instead, I worked really hard to get good grades, so I

could get into a good college, so I could work really hard to get a good job, so I could work really hard to get promoted, so I could work really hard to move up again...only to find myself conjuring up goofy anti-establishment cartoons as a way to stay awake in meetings.

We've all got an inner ten-year-old. You can honor her or you can ignore her. But once you invite her out to play, look out—you're going to have the best time of your life.

Do As I Say, Not As I Feel

Does the hand that rocks the cradle really rule the world? I don't know about that, but the nagging voice that says, "Pick up your dirty underwear," can often be heard from a few states away.

My own mom has been dead for more than ten years, and not only can I still hear her voice ringing in my ears, now it's starting to come out of my mouth, as well.

We all know mothers have a powerful effect on their children. Any shrink will confirm that if you tell your kids they're dumb, they'll probably grow up believing you.

But an increasing body of evidence suggests that while a mother's words carry a big impact, how she feels can play an even more powerful role in her child's physical and emotional health.

Best-selling author Dr. Christiane Northrup says, "Our bodies and beliefs were formed in the soil of our mothers' emotions, beliefs, and behaviors." It's not just how a mother feels about her children, but how she feels about herself that goes directly through to the next generation.

In her fascinating book, *Mother-Daughter Wisdom: Creating a Legacy or Personal and Emotional Health*, Dr. Northrup suggests, "Our skin, hair, heart, and lungs were nourished by her blood, blood that was awash with the neurochemicals formed in response to her thoughts, beliefs, and emotions. If she was fearful and anxious or deeply unhappy about her pregnancy, our bodies knew it."

Good lord, if that doesn't explain most of our neuroses I don't know what does. Our cells absorb our mother's negative thoughts, her cells took in her mother's—poor old great-grandma probably passed on enough negative baggage to fill up three seasons of Dr. Phil.

Using case studies, medical information, and her own personal life experience as both a daughter and mother, Dr. Northrup makes it very clear that children, especially daughters, take in "our mothers beliefs on a cellular level" throughout our lives. Said another way, you can feed your kids veggies every night of the week, but if you're walking around stressed out all the time, their little bodies are absorbing your angst right along with the Vitamin A in their greens.

If you've ever had a baby, you're probably flashing back to your pregnancy right now and feeling guilty about every time you cursed in traffic, fought with your husband, or, even worse, looked down at your enormous self and secretly wished the live person kicking your bladder would just go away, even if it was just for a night.

And if you're a mom, you're also probably beating yourself up about the days when you were in a bad mood, felt sorry for yourself, or prayed that your children would watch another fifteen minutes of Barney.

But before you throw yourself into the simmering cauldron of maternal remorse, consider this: Of the many emotions passed on from one generation to the next, guilt is probably one of the worst. The last thing you want to do is keep moving it down the line.

You'll be relieved to know that after years of medical practice, pain-staking research, and thousands of letters off her web site (DrNorthrup.com), Northrup confirms what many of us suspected all along: "There is no such thing as a perfect family that is completely free from unresolved emotional patterns."

With maternal lineages that may have included the atrocities of slavery or having your intestines contorted into a cone by a corset, it's pretty easy to see why our mothers' ancestors weren't passing along the joy. Knowing that your dad could sell you off to any available man for two chickens and a goat didn't exactly create a lasting legacy of female self-esteem.

Northrup suggests we often "give birth to personas that replace our true selves in an effort to win our mother's love." And she and I both agree with psychiatrist Carl Jung who said, "The greatest unconscious force in the lives of children is the unfulfilled dreams of their parents."

But like Aunt Sally's massive collection of salt and pepper shakers from every state in the union, just because you've been given something doesn't mean you have to keep it. And it doesn't mean you have to blame your mother for giving it to you either.

If I could wish for one thing next Mother's Day, it would be that the collective universe gave all mothers a real gift and agreed to let them off the hook.

No more guilt, no more shame, no more "Junior forgot to bring in his school picture money, and it's all your fault." Just overflowing love and acceptance for every mother alive that would reverberate for generations to come.

It's not the hand rocking the cradle that rules the world; it's the heart of the woman attached to it. Heal that, and we'll all breath a collective sigh of relief.

IO

Can You Blackberry Your Way to Happiness?

"The Internet is the Viagra of big business."

—JACK WELCH

Rat Racers, Back Away From the Starting Line

"The rat race is just going to have to survive with one less rat."

When Diane Keaton delivered that line in the movie *Baby Boom*, thousands of us secretly wished we could chuck it all away and move out to the country with her. No hassles, no stress, no traffic.

Commuting time isn't really the rat race. It's the race to get to the starting line of the rat race. And it's often the worst part of any job. Even if you don't have to face a daily grind, car time is consuming more of our lives than ever.

I recently saw an ad showing how you could hook an iPod up to a BMW. All the songs you've downloaded into your personal handheld music library can be blasted through the speakers of your Beamer. At first I got all excited. I have an iPod and I have every song ABBA ever sang loaded on it. Playing "Dancing Queen" everywhere I go surely would make my car time more enjoyable. But, alas, I quickly realized that much as I love my iPod, you also need a fancy BMW to make this system work. So I shall remain at the mercy of FM radio as I sit in my aging minivan, stuck in traffic yet again.

It is absolutely unbelievable that we human beings put up with this. There is not another species alive that would voluntarily choose to strap themselves into large hunks of moving metal, much less do it for endless hours at a time. Not that we don't go to great lengths to make our car time productive. Or, at least, less miserable. The diversions are endless.

There are the cell phone yakkers. Those of us who get so engrossed in our conversation we forget about things like turn signals. Then there are rock stars belting out tunes to their dashboard audience. Watch other commuters long enough, and you can tell who's listening to the same radio station you are. The people reading the paper are the ones who really blow me away. I guess they figure stop and go traffic is more stop than go, so why not catch up on the news?

I have one friend who actually used her breast pump every day during her afternoon commute. I swear I am not making this up. How she drove while she was hooked up to a portable milking machine is beyond me. I'm sure she gave a few truckers a thrill. But the breast pump company wouldn't be selling cigarette lighter car adaptors if my friend was the only one pumping and driving.

Of course, I'm the woman who's going to end up in the ER with a mascara wand sticking out of my eyeball because I ran off the side of the road while I was trying to put on my makeup.

All this time in the car is unnatural. It's taking us away from our real lives, and no amount of piped in music or mobile messaging makes it better. I know a lot of parents who say they have their best conversations with their kids while driving. And I have several friends who say drive time is the only time they can be alone. But isn't that like optimistic prisoners making the best of a bad situation?

Both of my kids weigh less than eighty pounds, so they have to sit in the back seat. If I want to have a meaningful conversation I've got to gauge their emotional response by looking in the rearview mirror. And as far as alone time goes, when your life gets so busy that driving is a respite, you need more than a long stretch of highway to get things back on track.

I hear companies are becoming more receptive to telecommuting and that people are trying not to be so dependent on automobiles. But try getting on the interstate at five o'clock—in Atlanta, that's a.m. or p.m.—and you'll realize our traffic problems are worse than ever.

Big picture answers take time. More community-based businesses, more sidewalks, less shopping, better urban planning, mass transit—solutions I hope we get to sooner rather than later. But as individuals, how much time we spend in our cars is a choice each of us can make. It's not as big a decision as who to marry or how many children to have, but it does have a significant impact on our daily lives.

At a certain point, there's only so much pain a lab rat will go through to get more cheese. You have to zap some of them a few times before they catch on. But eventually they all realize some races just aren't worth winning.

Honey, We Can All Hear You Now

Too much information. The annoying cell phone yakkers

used to be confined to their cars, but now they're roaming through Wal-Marts and Waffle Houses everywhere, treating the rest of us to an unwanted earful of information about their private lives.

They can't bear to pause their conversation at Starbucks, so the counter clerk has to decipher their order wedged in between meddling advice to their neighbor. "Marge, if you don't get little Carter in now—I'll have a grande, decaf, non-fat latte—he'll miss the cutoff for the four-year-old age group of the Future Neurosurgeons of America Club—and, uh, let me have one of those cinnamon chip scones."

They troll the aisles at Target, loudly recounting the lurid details of their sister-in-law's hysterectomy as they paw through the clearance toilet-seat covers.

And if you want to know how the average corporate flunky feels about their job, just go to the airport and stand next to somebody with one of those little neon blue contraptions in their ear. One click of a button and they assume that they're surrounded by an invisible, soundproof shield that somehow prevents the person standing two feet away from hearing their tirade against that nutty Sheila in accounting.

I'd tell them off, but I'm the woman in the middle of the food court with a headset perched in her ear, gesturing wildly as she tries to coach her husband through the proper carpool pickup procedure. "NO! NO! NO! The right lane is for drop-off, the left is for pick-up."

In defense of my annoying behavior, all I can say is, I'm a busy woman, and if God had wanted me to confine my conversations to my home, She wouldn't have sprinkled the earth with cell towers.

Readers often e-mail me wondering why, in my many

commentaries about the annoying behavior of humans, I've never gone after the intrusive cell phone chatters. Now, the truth is out: I can't call them out on the carpet because I'm one of the worst offenders of the lot. It would be treasonous to go after my own kind.

I envision my distraught family as the nightly news reports on a woman in a gold minivan seen careening off the overpass and plummeting to her death while clutching a cell phone. Bystanders at the scene say her last words were, "Can you hear me now?"

Yet aside from the obvious dangers, there are a few more insidious problems with all this constant talk time. First and foremost, it's hard to be fully present for your life when you've got a cell phone permanently glued to your ear. I shudder at the thought of how many times I've missed the chance to talk with my kids in the carpool line because I was busily boosting my productivity by cranking out calls on my cell. Glancing at all the other lunatics yakking away at traffic lights, I'm guessing I'm not the only one who reaches for the phone the second she puts her car in gear.

But even worse than missing important moments, constant cell phone use keeps your brain in permanent "on" mode. Like any good piece of equipment, the mind needs rest and quiet time to recharge. If we insist on jabbering during every waking moment, the little gears inside our brain are going to eventually explode.

I may be the queen of multitasking, but when your hairdresser has to wrench the phone from your hand to keep you from getting electrocuted while you're submerged in the shampoo sink, it's probably time to give it a rest.

So give your mouth and your mind a break. Take a deep

breath, put your phone on vibrate, and enjoy the world around you.

I promise I won't call.

Naked on the Net—It's a Good Thing

Big brother is watching, and I, for one, couldn't be more delighted. My days of dashing out for the paper in my ratty robe may be gone forever because, thanks to Google, satellite pictures of my home are up on the Web for all the world to see.

The Internet phenom, www.Earth.Google.com, known as a 3-D interface to the planet, allows you free access to satellite images of just about anywhere. If you didn't know about it before, feel free to curse me for telling you, because once you open the site you'll be up all night clicking on everything from the house where you grew up to the Eiffel Tower.

Too cheap to take the kids to Niagara Falls? Fly in via satellite, and you'll feel like you're riding the Maid of the Mist boat under the falls without even getting wet.

Like driving past your old boyfriend's house, but afraid of getting caught? Zoom in on the Web, and see what's parked in his drive. Actually, you probably won't be able to tell if he finally hauled that old Chevy to the dump. The Earth Google photos aren't in real time. They were taken via satellite some time during the last three years. But you don't have to be Steve Jobs or Bill Gates to make the technical leap and realize that if we can view still photos of your house on the Web today, by the end of next summer, we'll probably be able to watch live as you cut the grass. If the thought of others seeing you curse the starter on your mower with sweat dripping down your tube top makes you feel uncomfortable, you're not alone. Many believe that this capability is further evidence of how technology is stripping away our privacy and taking society down the tubes.

I'm as creeped out as the next person at the thought of a drooling pervert watching me play catch with my kids.

But I'm beginning to wonder if the idea of everyone knowing more about everybody else is actually a step in the right direction. Pretty soon we'll all know how much everybody makes, whether they pick their nose while flipping burgers on the grill, and probably what they look like naked. And then, at last, all pretenses will be gone.

We won't worry about somebody reading our mail or the neighbors finding out that we let our two-year-old pee in the grass because we were too lazy to take them inside and put them on the big potty. Thanks to the Web, our lives will be an open book.

The late Boyd Clarke of Tom Peters Company said, "We're in the infancy of the Internet. Its invention is the equivalent of only a few other communication turning points since the dawn of time—the invention of the spoken word, the invention of the written word, and the invention of the printing press."

The spoken word allowed caveman Zorg to tell his brother, Ogg, about plans to go hunting with his new pal, Zug. A few scribbled words on papyrus enabled ancient Egyptians to form alliances by recording who was related to whom. And the printing press was how Ben Franklin and his pals dispersed the ideas that united the colonies for the American Revolution.

With each step up the communication ladder, people become more connected to each other and previously secret information becomes widely known.

It once was thought television was the final stop on the communication frontier. But while TV may have altered the fabric of daily life, it was merely laying the groundwork for more sweeping changes that were yet to come. TV's scripted situations and entertaining images got us used to having strangers inside our homes. And reality shows have now anestheticized us to the gross-ness, humiliation, and angst of real life on planet Earth. With an entire generation raised beside a flickering screen, TV prepared our culture for what the Internet is now enabling us to do: get up close and personal with people we've never met.

The endless information on the Web may mean that you now know more about your disease than your doctor, and thanks to www.ConsumerReports.org, car buying will never be the same. But the truly transformative power of the Internet isn't just our access to data—it's our access to each other.

For better or for worse, we're at the tipping point of a radical societal change. The world is getting smaller, and we're getting more connected every day.

I personally think it's a good thing. It's going to be pretty hard to hate a guy half a world away when his video blog shows how much he loves his kids. And with satellites watching us all, it will be harder for the evil guys to find a place to hide.

Just like holding up a mirror up to a toddler, the Internet can be a way for people around the globe to take a closer look at ourselves. I only wonder if we'll like what we see.

Who Are These Weirdos in my House?

My computer crashed, my TIVO broke, and strangers have

invaded my home. The universe must be sending me a message.

First, my trusty laptop bit the dust after an untimely three-foot fall on concrete. My hard drive was fried, and my address book and e-mails vaporized faster than I could say, "What's backup?" So I shipped it off for repair and found myself computerless for the first time in seven years.

Six hours later, lightning zapped my TIVO. Just as I was about to discover who was getting booted off *American Idol*—flash, crack, boom!—it was gone. I not only missed the dramatic moment of pop star tension, now I've got to wait a week for a new machine.

No Web to surf. No e-mails to answer. No digitally recorded "must see TV" at my beck and call. So I did what any electronics addict would do: I went into painful withdrawal, shakes and all. By the end of the first day my keyboard-addicted fingers frantically were tapping on my desk like a three-pack-a-day smoker trying to quit without the patch.

With no gadgets buffering me from the happenings in my own home, I looked around and began to wonder—who are these people?

They act like they live here, but I don't remember anybody in my house being so old. Last time I looked up, I had two cute little kids and was married to a dashingly handsome man barely out of his thirties.

Who is this middle-aged guy? And who are the two blonds in hip huggers always asking me for a ride? Could I have been so distracted by my constant stream of electronic stimulation that my family grew up while I wasn't looking?

Their requests for food, money, and marital attention

sound like the background buzz I often heard outside my office door. But patiently listening to them, without wishing they would hurry up and finish, helped me get to know them better than my former strategy of waving them away so I could get back to work. And looking directly into their faces is much more interesting than catching their profiles reflected in the light of a digital screen.

Freed from electronic distractions I rediscovered my family, and they are a grand crew indeed. But after a few rounds of roasting marshmallows and talking about our feelings, we found ourselves back on the couch wondering what was on TV.

And that's when the real weirdos began showing up.

And this second crew of strangers aren't long lost family members. They are bizarre, insidious creatures with only one goal: They want to enslave the family I just reconnected with. They'd been lurking in the background, and the second our digital video recorder went down, they pounced.

My TIVO-trained family—who once zipped through commercials so fast the Barbies, breakfast cereals, and burritos blurred into blobs of color that would make a brand manager weep—is now transfixed by ads. And the cast of characters hawking everything from cell phones to cellulite cream is beginning to work its marketing magic on our minds.

Skinny blonds with the whitest teeth you've ever seen; hip skateboarders upping their cool quotient by chugging caffeine shooters in a can; and children so happy you'd swear their fast food meals came with a real live clown.

The strangers are coming forth by the thousands, wiggling and jiggling, doing the Dance of Consumerism for all to see.

When my children didn't ask for much last Christmas I assumed it was because my anti- materialistic message finally had sunk in. One evening of "family-friendly" programming proved me dead wrong. Kids who were once happy with chalk and a jump rope are suddenly begging for so much molded plastic junk you'd think God Himself had told them it was the secret to eternal bliss. And my frugal husband, who previously thought a perfect car was one that was paid for, now feels the overwhelming urge to purchase what appears to be a pair of $40,000 leather recliners that go from zero to sixty in three seconds flat.

I'd like to say I'm immune to the marketers' messages, but those women with the new, sparkly hardwood floors look so happy. Who knew domestic joy was just a phone call away?

You know, that's the funny thing about electronics. The people coming into your home via coax cable can change the dynamics of your entire family. The good-looking ones in the ads can make you covet stuff you never knew existed. And "you've got mail" often feels like an urgent message, no matter who sent it.

Strangers come into your home every day. It's a shame when they distract you from the people you really want to know.

II

Are Stretch Marks the Badge of Personal Growth?

"In my sex fantasy, nobody ever loves me for my mind."

—NORA EPHRON

Where Have All the Young Moms Gone?
I'm registering my oldest child for her first year of middle school. After making my way around the school paying for her lunch card, finding her classes, and jostling through the halls with herds of other families, I find myself wondering— Who are all these middle-aged people?

Surely, they're not the other parents. Parents with kids the same age as mine are cute and young, like me. At first glance I assume this older crew is a bunch of really "experienced" teachers. But no, they seem to be escorting around pre-teens, paying for lunch cards, and buying school spirit wear just like I am.

I'd just come from the elementary school that morning where I registered my youngest child, so I knew the moms my age were cute, young, and wore really cool clothes. So who were these people? Finally, I turned into the sixth-grade hall and saw a group of parents who looked like me. Imagine my surprise when I discovered that the cute group of young women I assumed would be my new mom friends turned out to be a gaggle of first-year teachers!

As it slowly dawned on me that maybe I wasn't as young-looking as I thought, one of the fresh-faced teachers stepped forward to say hello. Turns out she was my neighbor's daughter. As she introduced me to the other teachers as "her mother's friend," my transformation to middle-aged frump was complete. I hadn't been a cool, young chick for years, but the last one to know it was me.

I can give you the feminist party line about brains and ability being more important than looks. I can tell my two daughters that basing your self-worth on your appearance is a losing proposition. And I can assure you that from a spiritual perspective, what's in your heart and your soul is what really makes you attractive to others.

And it all sounds good, until you start to feel old.

I don't care how much else you have going for you, losing your looks is hard. It happens gradually, but you tend to notice it all of a sudden. Like the first time somebody in a store calls you ma'am. Or when you go to your class reunion and wonder why everybody else looks so old. Or the moment you realize the cute young girls are the students, and you're now one of the middle-aged, faceless mothers.

I used to be offended when the guys on a road crew gawked at me. Now, I'm wondering why I'm not good enough for them. How did I get to be a forty-year-old mother who actually cares about what construction workers think of her? The truth is, life is a little bit easier when you go through it good-looking, and losing that edge is often hard to take.

As best I can tell, there are no physical benefits to aging. And while men may suffer the same physical aches and pains, it's we women whose egos take the biggest bruising as we get older. A grey-haired guy with a few extra pounds on him is distinguished, but a woman in the same condition just looks fat and old.

Yet there's a certain freedom that comes with getting older. When nobody cares how you look, you can arrange your life around more important matters.

At a certain stage everybody crosses the line from looking good to looking good for your age. If you were once a hottie, it can be a long, hard fall. And even those of us who were just average find it unsettling to be viewed as less than young.

It takes grace and confidence to handle it well. One day the world may change and a woman with lines in her face will be treasured for her wisdom and experience, but until that happens we don't have to buy into some superficial attitudes about aging.

Nature is all about balance. As the shine from your outer shell fades, the light from your inner self has more room to glow. Those cute, young moms registering their kindergarteners may look better in hip huggers than the older crowd. But you'll never grow as a person if you waste all your time wishing you were back in elementary school.

The Perfect Bump

Demi Moore showed off three, Sarah Jessica Parker tucked one behind a designer handbag, and Julia Roberts took hers on *Oprah*. It's the new celebrity status symbol, and the more diminutive, the better.

The jet set may covet mongo diamonds, but when it comes

to pregnancies, if you're a woman of status, the only accept-able size is extra small.

People magazine, a trusted source for much of my infor-mation, now refers to a pregnant belly as a "bump." As in, "Bikini-clad supermodel Claudia Schiffer shows off her bump while frolicking on the beach."

Bump! Who are these women? A bump is what I had *before* I got pregnant.

After a real live baby started growing in my belly, the only thing on my body that could still be called a bump were the zits produced from my rampant hormones. The rest of my body resembled the foothills of Tennessee, one big rolling mound after another.

A recent edition of *New York Magazine* reports chic women consider the perfect pregnancy one where you can't tell from the rear the woman is even pregnant. I guess I'm just a red-neck from Georgia because I thought the perfect pregnancy is one where you get to eat mac 'n cheese every day and your husband graciously fetches you as much toffee ice cream as you deem medically necessary. I also thought the point of being pregnant was to grow a healthy baby, not look like a model while you were doing it.

For some bizarre reason we have now decided that preg-nancy, in its natural form, is an unwomanly and certainly unprofessional state of being. It's rather telling that the words, "You don't look pregnant," are considered one of the best compliments you can pay a woman who's expecting.

Pregnancy is the last stop on the control freak parade. We've conquered body odor, we've waxed ourselves hairless, and now we're going to prove that we can gestate without any evidence whatsoever.

I'm all for good nutrition during pregnancy, and I know there are some women out there who come by their pregnant thinness naturally. But for every one of those, there are twenty-five, or probably more like 105, others comparing themselves to some TV nymph or a size 2 runway model with a fake belly strapped to her front, hawking dresses for A Pea in the Pod.

Trying to maintain a perfect figure during pregnancy can be done, but it's a bit like trying to maintain your sanity during motherhood: It's completely unnatural. Pregnancy is one of Mother Nature's first big wake-up calls, a not-so-gentle reminder that you can't control everything. You never really could, but when your previously perky hair loses its bounce and your body starts to emit strange noises while you sleep, most of us realize there's something at stake here beyond vanity and ego. And life isn't all about you or how you look.

Pregnancy is the start of a long, rocky road in which personal grooming and TV-inspired visions of perfection take a backseat to the greater good. Weight gain and snorting at inopportune moments are merely a prelude of things to come. Trying to keep your body from doing what it's naturally programmed to do is as counterproductive as trying to make an active two-year-old wear white and sit still for a picture.

The truth is, you can swear off carbs, wear designer duds through the whole nine months, and decorate up your nursery with hand-painted puffy clouds fit for an angel, but no matter how you try to pretty it up, the natural end to a pregnancy is not a pink-cheeked Gerber baby. If you're lucky, that's the prize you get later, after six months of no sleep and nonstop breast-feeding. The natural culmination of a nine-month pregnancy is you thrashing about, half-naked, making guttural sounds while your body defies the laws of physics by pushing a human being out of somewhere you never dreamed could open that wide. (Sorry to be so graphic, but I don't make up the facts; I just report them.)

For those of you who haven't had children, in the spirit of full disclosure, I should also tell you that tummies almost never go back. And as much as you might like to think of your breasts as fashion accessories, Mother Nature actually intended for them to be functional feeding items that deflate upon use. It's all part of the grand plan, and it can be a beautiful thing if you let it.

Pregnancy affects your whole life and your whole body. There's no part of you that isn't changed forever. Once you quit caring about how you look from the rear, you can pay attention to the miracle happening right in front of you.

12

Can You Change a Person by Honking?

"Nothing so needs reforming as other people's habits."

—MARK TWAIN

Judging the Action-Packed Game of Parenting

Peer pressure parenting—an attempt to make other people's children behave simply by shooting their parents a dirty look. It never works, but it's practiced every day by busybodies in shopping malls and Chuck E. Cheeses across the land.

My favorite scenario is the crying-baby-on-the-airplane routine. As a former tot-toting traveler, I've been on the receiving end of this one, and I can tell you exactly how it works. You board the plane dragging along a diaper bag stuffed with every available device to keep your child content: bottles, animal crackers, diapers, a change of clothes, and enough Beanie Babies to start a stuffed animal zoo. Yet, despite your best efforts to keep her occupied, your child begins squalling and will not stop. As your infant screams in your ear, this prompts many of your fellow passengers to begin rolling their eyes and sighing loudly in your direction.

They seem to believe you either are deaf or you enjoy nonstop wailing at 35,000 feet. And they obviously are hoping that by giving you the evil eye, you will awaken to the fact that they are annoyed, and you will finally give your child the magic Be Quiet pill you have been hiding in your purse.

When this happened to me on one flight, I almost wanted to tell one well-suited businessman, "Thanks for the nasty look. I hadn't noticed she was crying, but now that you've alerted me, I guess I'll stop pinching her."

I'm just as annoyed with screaming, ill-mannered kids as the next person, but making their parents feel like scum never helps. In fact, it usually makes the situation worse. I can understand why childless people might think they are providing a public service by pointing out parenting errors in public. I myself was once so naive as to believe my children would never do that. But after a few "I WANT SKITTLES!" hissy fits in the checkout line, I realize that not everything is within a parent's control.

Although nasty looks and unsolicited advice from strangers may make you feel like the world—or at least everyone on the plane—thinks you're a bad parent, nothing makes you more defensive than criticism from your own parents.

I was pawing the clearance rack at Old Navy recently, and I saw how powerful a mother's disapproval of her child's parenting can be.

As I stood rummaging through the two-for-one T-shirts, I noticed a little girl about three-years-old whining to her mother for some glitter sandals. Her mother, who appeared to be about thirty, gave a tense "no," grabbed her child's hand, and marched her off in the other direction. Moments later, in a different part of the store, I saw the mother arguing with a fifty-ish woman who appeared to be her mother. With her little daughter standing a few feet away, ogling more merchandise, the younger woman barked defensively at her mother, "I said 'no'—doesn't that make you happy?"

Grandma narrowed her eyes into one of the most judgmental looks I've ever seen and snapped, "I'd be happy if you could make that child mind."

And with that the younger woman stomped over to her child, picked her up, heaved her into the cart, and all the negative energy from two generations of women descended down upon a three-year-old.

As the inevitable crying ensued, the older woman's nose wrinkled up even further. Her lips pursed even tighter, and her judgmental frown turned into an evil scowl. The younger mother, with her knuckles white from clenching the cart, hissed under her breath "Stop crying right now." And the unhappy trio made their way to the checkout.

It was all I could do not to stage an intervention right there, next to the clearance flip-flops. I didn't know whether to hug the kid, shoot an encouraging smile at the younger mother, or slap the older woman silly.

I have no idea how this family behaves in other circumstances. For all I know, this was just a bad day, and Grandma is usually as loving and giving as Olivia Walton. But I do know that when a parent is in the middle of a bad situation, it's the worst time to offer advice. And if that parent happens to be your child, the more judgmental you are of their parenting skills, the less likely you are to improve them.

I have to wonder what would have happened if, when things got tense, Grandma had offered support instead of criticism. What if she had hugged her daughter and said with a smile, "It's okay, honey, they all act like that sometimes?" Maybe her daughter could have calmed down, taken a deep breath, and responded with positive energy rather than channeling all her mother's negative junk.

The Wicked Witch of the Discount Jeans may think she's helping, but when it comes to the high stakes game of parenting, judges flashing scores from the sidelines only make the players choke.

Honk if I'm an Idiot!

Thank you for honking.

How stupid of me to pick the hottest day of summer to allow my car to break down in the middle of the road. I hadn't noticed the smoke spewing out of my engine, nor was I aware of the snaking line of traffic snarling at me for blocking their path. Now that your helpful honk has alerted me to the problem, I'll wave my magic dipstick and rectify this situation immediately, so that you will no longer be inconvenienced by my stupid behavior.

Once considered a warning signal, honking has become the high-speed equivalent of a dirty look. Actually, it's a bit more aggressive than a dirty look; it's sort of like a public dressing down. It lets the other person know what an idiot they are and reminds them not to do it again, especially in your presence.

The ferocity with which people lay on their horns these days leads me to think that they're not only trying to discipline their fellow drivers, but they're also trying to honk commands for proper motorist behavior. A minivan full of screaming kids takes too long placing their order at the drive-thru? Three short blasts tells their frazzled mother, "Lady, ask your stupid kids what they want before you get up to the clown's head."

A beat-up Ford Escort doesn't gun it fast enough the second the light turns green? Lay on the horn until the middle-aged minister heeds your message: "Hey, moron, quit daydreaming and get a car with better pick-up."

A huge white Pontiac pokes down a residential street at thirty-five miles per hour. Honk every two hundred feet to let the blue-haired driver know, "If you're gonna drive like a grandmother, get the hell off my street."

I'm just as impatient as the next person, and if I'm running late, it often seems like every other driver on the road is intentionally trying to get in my way. What with their unannounced left turns and the annoying way they slow down just to go right, you'd think nobody ever taught them how to drive. But as bothered as I am by the asphalt errors of others, I have to wonder if you can really change a person by honking at them?

Prior to street lights and headlights, automobile horns were originally intended to signal to the people (and horses) ahead that a car was approaching. An ad for an early car horn claimed, "You press as you steer, and your pathway is clear." Although the days of jauntily announcing your Model T's arrival via a quick squeeze of your bulb horn are over, many people believe it still works that way—that laying on the horn will get all the annoying people out of your way, leaving the roads and parking lots free for you and your perfect driving.

But while punching a button on your radio can shut up a shock jock and a quick squeeze of your garage remote magically makes the door respond to your every whim, pounding on your horn cannot make people behave the way you want them to.

So if you happen to see me careening across five lanes of traffic, chances are I've either fallen asleep, or I'm trying to reach a Happy Meal toy under the back seat, and a good loud blare is the appropriate response to keep me from killing myself and possibly you.

However, if I don't get my kids buckled in the car and pull out of your chosen parking space quickly enough, honking, or even politely tooting, isn't going to make me go any faster. And if my car is on fire in the middle of the freeway, it's a pretty safe bet that I already know. Your bleeping horn is only making matters worse.

Circle of Dumping: The Golden Rule in Reverse
THE DUMPER: Either you've been one, or you've been her victim.

The Dumper is the woman who drops her women friends the second a guy—any guy—shows up on the scene. She'll leave you in a bar, forget to give you the promised ride home from a party, or quit calling you altogether as long as Mr. Wonderful is around.

It's not only a crummy way to treat your girlfriends, but it's usually counterproductive in the mad scramble for the attention of the opposite sex.

My dear friend and dating expert, Lisa Daily, the author of *Stop Getting Dumped,* says, "What usually happens is— girl meets guy, girl drops friends so she can be on call 24/7 for guy, guy starts to suffocate from over-attention, guy drops girl, girl has no guy and no friends."

Male Dumpers are less common. But while leaving your

buddies in a bar for the mere prospect of female companionship may be considered acceptable behavior, men who consistently wimp out on poker night to see a chick flick pay a heavy price when they return to the pack.

"In a situation where a man has a chance to score with a woman he doesn't know, he is revered for leaving his friends at the bar. But if it's a woman he's been with for a while, he's ridiculed for the exact same behavior," says Daily.

She suggests that, "Ditching your friends when something better comes along doesn't just make you a bad friend, it makes you a karmic target for a king-size helping of the same."

It's no coincidence that the people who dump are the most likely to be dumped. It's sort of like the Golden Rule in reverse: Do it to others, and they'll do it to you. Many in the spiritual world have suggested that our traditional interpretation of the Golden Rule doesn't fully capture its true essence. It's not: "Do unto others as you would have them do unto you." It's actually: "When you do unto others, you do unto you."

How many times have we seen this concept play out?

We eradicated small pox. Yet, we hung on to the last little bit just in case we ever wanted to annihilate some future enemy. Now, the few vials floating around have put the entire country in peril. Diplomatic Decree: Intended future harm begets current bio-weapons terrorist threat.

Enron executives who gambled away their employees' futures for one more pull on the greed machine turned their own lives into a house of cards. The employees are broke, but the big guys are flat busted. Earnings Report: Gamble with other people's money, and your own future becomes a losing game of Russian roulette.

Statistics show that when a couple who cheated together gets married, there is a ninety-five percent chance one will cheat again. So the one who stabbed a former spouse in the back almost always gets stabbed in return. Love Lesson: If you betray someone, brace yourself, because you can count on someone betraying you.

And one of the best examples illustrating the circle of bad deeds comes from talk show host Angela Harrington Rice of WAIB in Atlanta who says, "The U.S. outlaws certain pesticides, but then we ship them off to foreign countries. They spray them on their vegetables and then send that same produce right back to us." Trade Formula: Poison out, poison in.

It's doesn't matter whether you're a country or an individual—what goes around comes around. Judgmental people always feel judged. Critical people wind up being criticized. Rude people never get good service. And dumpers get dumped on.

When are we going to learn? Whether it's a universal truth, a direct hit from the Big Guy upstairs, or concrete proof that we are all directly linked as part of the same divine humanity, when we treat other people badly, it always comes back. And usually comes back worse than we sent it out.

I wonder how we might act if we stayed conscious of that fact, knowing every time we did something wrong to someone else, we were literally doing it to ourselves as well. There probably would be a lot fewer friends left alone at the bar.

If you've even been the victim of a Dumper, or been slighted in some other nasty way, it's tempting to help the universe along by showing the perpetrator a little Golden

Rule action of your own. Don't bother—the laws of karma like to work alone.

But if you plot revenge, you'd better dig two graves.

13

Can Sponge Bob Get You into Mensa?

*"If you bungle raising your children,
I don't think whatever else you do well
matters very much."*

—JACQUELINE KENNEDY ONASSIS

Sponge Bob, Monet, and PTA

Want your kids to do better on standardized tests? Plunk them in front of the TV and head out to PTA.

In his best-selling book, *Freakonomics: A Rogue Economist Explores the Hidden Side of Everything,* Steven D. Levitt asks and answers a simple question—what makes a perfect parent?

Levitt, who "studies the riddles of everyday life," offers data-driven conclusions about the art of parenting that will change your perceptions forever. Using a regression analysis on mountains of data from a federal study, Levitt and co-author Stephen Dubner (Freakonomics.com) reveal the parenting factors that correlate with test scores. Among their many startling findings is that a parent's involvement in PTA does matter, but whether a child frequently watches television has no bearing on their scores whatsoever.

Being a PTA mom whose kids are developing a deep relationship with Sponge Bob while I work the phone tree, I was greatly relieved to think that I was actually upping their IQ. However, Leavitt and Dubner burst my bubble by clarifying that the correlation "probably indicates that parents with a strong relationship to education get involved in PTA, not that their PTA involvement somehow makes their children smarter."

Damn.

Some of the other factors that correlate to test scores are, not surprisingly, the education level of the parents, whether English is spoken in the home, and if a lot of books are around. But things that demonstrate no correlation to test scores are an intact family, moms not working between birth and kindergarten, and regular trips to museums.

"It isn't so much a matter of what you do as a parent, it's who you are," the authors suggest.

But wait a minute—I thought those expensive clarinet lessons would stimulate Junior's mind, so he could break 700 on the math SAT. And shouldn't that Sculpting for Tots class insure that little Bethany was a shoo-in for the gifted-and-talented program?

Sorry, no dice. Levitt's research confirmed what many of us slacker moms have hoped all along: Cultural enrichment may create a more educated child, but it will not raise her IQ. The good news is if you're feeling guilty because you didn't play the baby Mozart tapes or quit your job so you could take your kids to art galleries every week, you're off the hook.

But the bad news is if your kids test well and you were

hoping your parenting merit badge was in the mail, forget it. Your brilliant offspring owe more of their intelligence to the chromosomes passed down from Grandpa Fred and Grammy Buella than you doing the Better Baby flash cards six hours a day.

The lesson here? Much of the prevailing trend toward hyper-parenting is wasted effort.

The current cultural norm goes something like this: The harder you work at parenting, the smarter your kids will be. Academic achievement is directly proportional to parenting skills. So when your kid gets an *A* in math, your parenting score is one hundred percent.

But if that idea is completely wrong and your child's IQ is predetermined, does parenting really matter?

Of course it does. It matters when it comes to shaping values, work habits, and ethics, not ratcheting up test scores. Those brilliant ancestors of yours didn't waste their time trying to produce the perfect kid. They believed that parenting was a moral obligation to society.

I wonder what would happen in today's world if, instead of spending our time and money on Baby Trig classes and computer-enhanced learning systems, we accepted our children's IQs and focused our efforts on teaching them how to use it? If your child is brilliant (as I'm sure yours is) that means your job as a parent is not only more difficult, but more important. After all, Hitler had an above average IQ, but nobody cares much about how well he did in school.

As a mom who's convinced she is raising future world leaders, I've come to realize that while an SAT prep class may raise their scores a few points, spending a Saturday at a homeless shelter teaching them the value of compassion will have a bigger planetary payoff. My main job as a parent is to create character, not boost brains.

IQ is one of the many cards your children are dealt at birth. Their parents are one of the others. One will stay pretty much the same over the course of their lives, but improvements in the other can make all the difference in the world.

Fatty, Fatty Two-By-Four Coming Through the Lunchroom Door

Pizza, pasta, and a big, soft pretzel. If you scrape the sauce off the pizza, it's an all-white, flour lunch.

Tired of shopping for healthy alternatives and trying to cook real food? Do what the school systems do: Load your family up on empty carbs, and watch the fun begin.

Sure, you'll have to scrape the kids off the ceiling during the early afternoon sugar spike, and the 2:00 p.m. drop in serotonin makes it hard to keep their attention. But toss them a few pieces of candy during the day, and they'll hold up just fine. It will be hard to sleep at night after all that sugar, and they'll probably struggle with diet-related illnesses for the rest of their lives, but just think of all the time and money you'll save.

No more slicing and dicing vegetables. No paying the big bucks for organic. Heck, if you play it right and buy in bulk, you can get enough hormone-injected, deep-fried nuggets to host an entire Cub Scout meeting. Forget the long term—go for the quick fix.

A hundred years ago only rich people could afford processed sugar; now it's the opposite. The BMW set are the ones who shop at Whole Foods, but you can get a burger and fries on your way out of Wal-Mart. The Centers for

Disease Control and Prevention says diet-related illnesses have now surpassed cigarette smoking as the No. 1 cause of preventable deaths.

But we don't need statistics to tell us we're unhealthy. Look around. Planes now offer seat belt extenders. A few hours of yard work leaves us so worn out we can't get up the next day. Diet books sell like crazy, but never seem to work. And we're raising a generation of kids who would rather spend their afternoons chomping on chips in front of the computer than playing outside.

How many fat kids were in your grade school? Usually it was just one, a lonely kid everyone in the class probably should go back and apologize to. But fat kids aren't the outcasts anymore; they're the new norm.

We talk about the epidemic of childhood obesity, but I don't see us doing a whole lot about it. The daily starch festival at your local public school cafeteria may have Dr. Atkins rolling in his grave, but it's the natural result of the absolutely unnatural way we produce, promote, and distribute food.

Chef Ann Cooper, author of *Lunch Lessons: Changing the Way We Feed Our Children,* says, "Many school lunch programs are dominated by processed and packaged foods."

Schools have to serve kids, cheap, fast, and easy. They turn to empty carbs for the same reason we parents do— it works.

But isn't it rather bizarre to spend six hours a day teaching kids academic skills and then give them only twenty minutes to bolt down a junk food lunch? Let's be honest, a person can live a fabulous life without ever knowing who won the War of 1812, but if you don't know how to eat right, you're in for some pretty big problems.

Chef Ann, who calls herself a "lunch lady on a mission," provides schools and parents with nutrition guides, sample lunches, and recipes at LunchLessons.org. But she's only one person; the only way things will really change is if the community decides our kids deserve something different.

Coke machines as a school profit center, candy as behavior incentives, and high starch fillers to keep meal costs down may work in the short term, but these kids are going to need a crane to get them off the sofa if we stay on this program.

Mother Nature had a plan. You grew your own food and burned off more calories planting it than you gained by eating it. You had to run after your meat to catch it, so it stayed skinny and so did you. And kids played so hard, they were too hungry at dinnertime to turn up their nose at green stuff.

If nobody had ever tasted pepperoni pizza, we wouldn't know what we were missing. And if there were no drive-thrus, it would have never dawned on us that you could get a super-size meal for three bucks in under two minutes.

But just because that stuff is out there, it doesn't mean we have to take it.

The kids scarfing down the carb fest in the cafeteria are going to be paying your Social Security one day. It'd be a shame if they were too sick to work, and all you had for retirement was a big wad of pizza dough.

The Cinderella Syndrome is Plagued with Flakey Glitter

Seems like every woman either wants to be a princess or she's trying to raise one. At Disney World, Cinderella's Coach is the best-selling add-on for weddings. For a mere $2,500, princess-wannabes can spend two hours in a glass coach imitating a woman who married royalty simply because her foot fit into a glass shoe.

In my own house, Princess Barbie goes to make-believe balls every afternoon, while Animal Doctor Barbie sits alone on the shelf, all but abandoned by her seven-year-old owner.

One quick stroll through the mall and you'll find more pre-teen girls sporting bubble gum pink T-shirts with glitter script proclaiming "I'm a Princess" than you can shake a scepter at. I'm not quite sure when divas went out of style, and I very rarely hear anybody say she wants to be queen. But the shine on the princess fairytale remains as sparkly as ever.

Queens and divas may use their power or talent to get their way, but a princess just shows up and looks good. And who wouldn't want to be rewarded for that? My twelve-year-old daughter says, "Queens have to run the country and worry about politics and all that stuff. Princesses go shopping, wear jewelry, and get their picture in *People* magazine."

A life of shopping and posing for *People*? Sounds more like Paris Hilton to me.

In spite of several real life examples to the contrary, many of us continue to believe that princesses—the showbiz version or the bluebloods—have it made. Yet we need look no further than Di and Fergie to see all the wide-brim hats and designer shoes in the world can't fill a lonely heart.

Sure, they had problems with eating disorders, unavailable husbands, extramarital affairs, and meddling in-laws. But I suspect their biggest obstacle to happiness was a lack of purpose. When your primary role is to look good for your country and wave to your adoring fans, it only takes a few trips down the parade route before your smile becomes fake.

But kids aren't the only ones who mistakenly believe a tiara will guarantee them a lifetime of bliss.

It's a common adult misconception as well. We often think if we had tons of money, and a little fame to go with it, all our cares would be washed away. We would be freed from our responsibilities, and with no pressure in our lives, we'd be happy 24/7. But how many strung-out celebrities and divorcing royals do we have to see before we finally get the message? A life with no meaningful purpose slowly but surely drives a person insane.

Britney and Paris may have enough Manolos to fill the castle moat, but they sure don't look very content to me. Like it or not, we human beings are wired to make meaningful contributions. And when we don't do it, our lives become pretty miserable.

I'm not suggesting we're hardwired for drudgery. Pushing papers around a desk all day isn't going to make you feel any better than twenty-three sets of jewel-encrusted opera gloves. Yet the idea that a life of riches and rest will make you happy has been proven wrong time and time again.

Nazi concentration camp survivor Victor Frankl claimed we should "balance the Statue of Liberty on the East Coast with a Statue of Responsibility on the West Coast." The widely quoted idea has also been attributed to Scott Peck, author of the mega best-selling *A Road Less Traveled*.

As much as we may think we'd prefer total freedom over any responsibility, life experiences taught both Frankl and Peck that a satisfying life includes both. Both men suggest that much of human suffering stems from our misguided belief that we were not meant to do any work and from our resistance to take full responsibility for our lives and emotions.

When you're feeling overwhelmed with life, it's easy to think that a white horse, a golden coach, and a dashing prince are the answers to all your dreams. And if that didn't happen for you, it's tempting to hope your daughter will have better luck. Though, I have to wonder how the current generation is going to fare when the glitter on their pink T-shirts starts to flake off. Raising a pampered princess, or aspiring to be one yourself, only perpetuates a plan that never works.

If you're really looking for that happily ever after, consider modeling yourself after a queen—someone who gracefully takes responsibility for her kingdom and still gets to wear nice clothes. A queen's crown may be a bit heavier than a princess's tiara, but that's because the jewels inside it are real.

Putting "What" Before "Who" is a Backwards Approach

"What are you going to be when you grow up?"

This is a horrible question to ask children because it implies that what you do is who you are. It's probably also the reason we grownups ask each other, "What do you do?" the second after we're introduced.

The "I am my job description" mentality is a uniquely American concept. We want a quick label for everything, and we mistakenly assume that knowing what someone does explains who they are. Yet how many people do you know truly love what they do, much less consider it a full reflection of who they are as a human being?

Ask adults what they want to be when they grow up, and if they're honest, most will tell you they don't have a clue. I think the reason so many of us are confused about our life purpose is we use the wrong starting point. We look at jobs and careers and try to decide which one we might be good at, or which ones pay the most, but many of us have never taken the time to figure out what our true talents are. It's hard to do, and it usually takes help.

It absolutely blows my mind how little attention is paid to self-discovery in school and early training. I spent twelve years in grade school, four years in college, and five years in a management training program trying to get really good at the things other people said were important.

It wasn't until I took the Myers-Briggs personality test at age thirty that I realized how unsuited I was for just about everything I was trying to do. A simple test found on zillions of web sites gave me more life guidance than any boring career fair ever did.

You can investigate jobs, hobbies, and volunteer opportunities all you want, but until you're clear on who you are, you'll never find the right fit. And you'll cheat yourself out of discovering what you're really great at.

Before you jump to the conclusion you're not great at anything or what you really love isn't going to pay the bills, give yourself some time and space to do some conceptual thinking. Think about the times when you've been totally in the moment. You know, those activities where you're so immersed in something you lose all track of time. Understanding exactly why that is so engaging for you is the key to discovering your own unique talents and skills.

Whether it's writing letters, playing miniature golf, talking on the phone, watching old movies, or making up silly games with your kids, you need to do more of it, because chances are you're really good at it.

Often when we're intuitively good at something, it comes so naturally to us we don't even realize it's a marketable skill. It took ten years of comments about my hilarious Christmas letters before it finally dawned on me that I could be a writer.

Successful and happy lives are built on knowing who you are and making the most of the gifts you've been given. If you're in a proactive career mode, do yourself a favor and read *Do What You Are* by Paul Tieger and Barbara Barron-Tieger before you send out your resume. It will be the best $20 you ever spend on your profession development, and it could save you years of floundering around in jobs you're not suited for.

Whether your currently working or not, I encourage you to take the Tiegers' online personality test at www.PersonalityType.com. It will give you new insight into yourself and how you relate to the world around you.

And I think every parent alive should read the Tiegers' other best-seller, *Nurture by Nature*, a book that single-handedly shifted my entire perspective on a certain shy four-year-old—a young lady who eventually blossomed into an amazing thirteen-year-old once her mother quit trying to change her.

The next time somebody asks my kids, "What do you want to *be* when you grow up?" I hope they'll be able to respond, "Just a bigger, better version of who I am right now." And I hope by the time they're officially grown up, they will have put the energy into discovering who that is.

Mom's on Auto Pilot, Look Out

Her eyes quickly scan the horizon. She locks in on her target, she takes aim, she shoots—and she scores! The second-grade chess club sponsor falls to the floor, writhing in pain. It's another victory for Helicopter Mom. Her mission:

Annihilate anyone who dares to make life less than perfect for her little Tommy.

"Helicopter parents" is the new tag line for all those moms and dads who hover in the back of the classroom, micromanage the gift wrap sale, or try to coach a T-ball game from the stands. They take over every aspect of their kids' lives, leaving a trail of bloody and battered guidance counselors, choir directors, teachers, and coaches in their wake.

Woe unto the Brownie leader who forgets to give Muffy her full minute during circle time.

A helicopter mom's job is to make sure her kids don't experience a single moment of pain, frustration, or disappointment during their childhoods. For some unfathomable reason, she believes this will somehow better prepare her child for life as an adult.

A few decades ago, getting an *A* in parenting meant keeping your kids fed, clothed, and alive until they reached age eighteen. Volunteering to lead the Daisy troop netted you bonus points. And if you paid for college, well, you were going above and beyond.

But things have changed. Somewhere between the "Go out back, and choose your own switch for your whippin'" years and the current "Now, Conner, you know you can only have one new X-Box game a week," parenting shifted from disciplining kids to serving them.

I'm just as guilty as the next parent of wanting to right all the wrongs of my own childhood by trying to make things perfect for my kids. But if we constantly run interference for them, how will they ever learn to manage alone?

In fairness, part of the micromanaging mommy trend is due to safety and proximity issues. Kids can no longer freely roam a neighborhood full of tightly knit friends, so Mom has no choice but to arrange a play date and drive them over to Billy's house.

Electronic apron strings also play a role in parental over-involvement. Cell phones, e-mail, and instant messaging start out as a way to keep tabs on a teen, but the constant communication habit often means Mom and Dad don't unplug when Suzie heads off to college.

A *Wall Street Journal* article reports that HR directors are actually having to field calls from recruits' parents wanting to discuss the benefit package being offered to their working child. If my mom had called my first boss at Procter & Gamble, I think he would have retracted the offer.

But I suspect the root of the helicopter parent problem has nothing to do with safety, logistics, or even better stock options. The real issue is love. Many of us look back on our own childhoods with some sadness. We think about the time we had to face off with a bully or deal with an unfair teacher alone. We remember longing for the cool clothes or a senior trip to the beach. And our faces still burn at the humiliation of being cut from the team or losing the race for class vice president.

It's only natural that we would want to protect our kids from the same sorrows. But perhaps our pain didn't come from losing the big game. Perhaps it was because nobody taught us we were special in spite of it.

The line between supporting and suffocating is blurry at best, and I've certainly erred on both sides of it. But the reality is, you're not trying to create a perfect childhood—you're trying to create a functioning adult.

Our job as parents is to provide the gas, not fly the plane.

14

Why isn't Poccahontas President of the United States?

"We are the ones we have been waiting for."

—HOPI PRAYER

Does Your Mamma Know You're Acting Like That?
"They're evil, soulless killers. They despise our way of life, and they want to destroy anything they can't understand." This isn't an American talking about the terrorists. It's what the average person in the Middle East thinks about us.

It's been over five years since 9/11, and many of us are more confused about world politics than ever.

Before September 11, most of us were going about our daily lives with the unconscious belief that world events didn't really affect us. International news was bewildering, often boring, and didn't seem too relevant in the scope of our individual lives. Keeping up with what regime overthrew another and what the leaders were telling their people didn't seem like a big priority when you had a mountain of bills and nobody in the house had any clean underwear.

But 9/11 proved that what people think halfway around

the world does affect us. Like it or not, we are part of a global community, one world filled with other human beings who have just as much right to this planet as we do. And we can't depend on sound bites and stereotypes to help us figure them out.

People were appalled at the American treatment of the prisoners in Abu Ghraib several years ago. But it's a logical outcome of the culture we've created. When you refer to an entire nation as an "Axis of Evil" with no soul, it's not too big a leap to figure out why the people we trained as killers might regard their depersonalized captives as subhuman.

I come from a long line of military men, so I know the last thing we need on the front lines is a bunch of softies who want to think through the human implications of everything they're doing. But most of us aren't on the front lines, so we owe it to ourselves to contemplate the bigger issues.

Evil does exist in the world, but it comes in pretty small numbers. What come in bigger numbers are aimless followers. People who are hungry, hurt, lonely, and scared will follow just about anybody who seems to have a plan.

Hitler couldn't have turned a nation against the Jews if Germany had been fat and happy after World War I. And the Holy Wars wouldn't have been able to recruit soldiers if people had felt fully confident about their own spot in heaven.

Fear is always the impetus for following a lunatic. Even a half-baked leader can turn fear into action. Because pointing the finger at those evil "other guys" is a lot easier than asking people to calm down and figure out solutions to their own problems. When people feel persecuted and wronged, the last thing they're going to do is take a reflective look in the mirror.

It's a model that's as old as time: fear to anger to action. Two-year-olds do it and so do grownups.

People say the definition of insanity is doing the exact same things over and over and expecting a different result. I don't pretend to be a foreign policy expert, but I do notice patterns of human behavior. And I'm seeing the same fears take humanity down the tube time and time again.

The cynic in me thinks testosterone might have something to do with it. But we women are the ones sitting around letting it happen. We gave birth to every one of those shouting angry men who have incited people to violence. And we've also given birth to every single person they've killed.

Call me naive, but I doubt very many of us endured the pain of labor to watch them do this to each other. Moms have no problem intervening when one kid smacks another over the head in a fight for a plastic toy. We read books and talk with other mothers about the best way to handle the situation because we have a vested interest in turning out the best children we possibly can.

But what would happen if we applied that same effort, wisdom, and thought to the world outside our own children?

Politics and world affairs do apply to us. And by *us*, I mean every woman on either side of the globe. These boys are playing a dangerous game, and it's time for somebody's mother to step in and stop them.

Gaggle of Grandma's in the Galley

"In our every deliberation, we must consider the impact of our decisions on the next seven generations."

A quote from a forward-thinking politician? I wish. It's an Iroquois Confederacy maxim that has been used for centuries by Native American leaders as a way to evaluate decisions.

If ever there was a time to consider the impact of our decisions on future generations it's during an election. Choosing leaders isn't easy, and I try not to make a practice of telling people who they should vote for. We have more than enough people shouting at us about that.

However, what I do suggest is that the next time you vote, you turn away from the negative campaign ads. Put aside other people's opinions, and take some time to carefully collect your own thoughts on the matter.

Forget about who your parents voted for, which party you've supported in the past, what your neighbors think, who your minister suggested, or even who your spouse is voting for. Take a few minutes to think about what you want for our country. Not just for yourself, but for the generations to follow.

One of the criteria many people consider when deciding which candidate to vote for is how their plans will personally affect us. Are they for this or against that? Will I pay more taxes or less? Will they expand my pet causes or stomp on them? Do their religious beliefs match my own? But where would we be right now if our forefathers had put their own interests first?

It might surprise you to know that much of the principles embodied in the Declaration of Independence were based on the Great Law of Peace that united five Native American tribes. Thomas Jefferson, the author of the Declaration of Independence, and his primary editor, Benjamin Franklin, both were avid students of the Native American governing model. Franklin's posterity clause, found in the Preamble, which states that our descendants are guaranteed the "Blessings of Liberty" was derived from the Iroquois concept of providing for the seventh generation.

Native American chiefs considered the generations to come their most important constituents. Leaders were appointed for life, and, in a stroke of brilliance, a group of elder women, the "Clan Mothers," was chosen to watch closely over all meetings. Their job was to ensure the interests of the seventh generation were being well represented.

As much as I'd love to imagine how proceedings in Congress might change if they had a group of overprotective grandmothers constantly looking over their shoulders, I don't see it happening any time soon. And I doubt the Supreme Court justices are going start polling moms in the carpool line before they go into chambers for their next decision.

Today's politicians are more concerned with keeping their base of supporters happy enough or at least confused enough to get themselves reelected. And they're more likely to spend their time tending to the interests of whoever paid for their TV ads than the well-being of people who will be living a couple hundred years from now.

But that's where you come in. We may not have anyone in our government officially appointed to look after the interest of the next seven generations, but I have to believe we're smart enough to think about issues from that perspective ourselves.

What do you want it to mean seven generations from now when your heirs say, "I'm an American?"

There are two important days during every election cycle: Election Day itself and the day after. Election Day is when we're called to look beyond our own personal concerns and think about what we want for our great-grandchildren's great-grandchildren.

The day after an election is when we face an even more difficult challenge. That's when we need to put aside our political differences and work toward the common good. The phrase "burying the hatchet" actually entered idiomatic English from the Iroquois Great Law. The Native Americans knew they would accomplish more by uniting than they would wasting their energies on inner tribal war.

Sitting Bull said, "Let us put our minds together and see what life we can make for our children." Giving "careful consideration to the interests of the next seven generations" was the American way long before our ancestors showed up on the scene. Are we going to embrace the tradition or abandon it?

Is a Sliver of the Pie Too Much to Ask For?
Forget candy and flowers, next Mother's Day, I want something more.

It's big, and it's expensive, but I'm worth it. It'll take more effort than serving me some runny eggs on tray with a sappy card. And it's a bit more pricey than a day at the spa. But after birthing two kids—one of them a nine-pounder with no epidural, thank you very much—it's the least my family can do.

I want what the creator of Mother's Day asked for in 1870 but never got: peace.

Long before it became an homage to consumerism, Mother's Day was originally intended to be a Mother's Day for Peace. In a fiery speech condemning the carnage that she witnessed while nursing the wounded during the American Civil War, noted Unitarian Julia Ward Howe, who wrote the "Battle Hymn of the Republic," declared:

> Arise all women who have hearts, say firmly: Our sons shall not be taken from us to unlearn all that we have been able to teach them of charity, mercy, and patience. We women of one country will be too tender of those of another country to allow our sons to be trained to injure theirs. In the name of womanhood and of humanity; take counsel with each other as the means whereby the great human family can live in peace.

Howe failed in her attempt to get formal recognition of a Mother's Day for Peace. And by the time President Woodrow Wilson declared the first national Mother's Day in 1914, the call for peace and patience had been replaced by bon-bons and breakfast in bed.

I'm all for pampering, but I think it's time we mothers started asking for something more. It's time we asked for something that truly honors the work we do on this planet. It's time we asked the world to keep our babies safe.

Peace is as patriotic as Mom's apple pie. That's why mothers across America deliver "peace pies" to their legislators each year the week before Mother's Day, asking that peace and nonviolence be given a piece of the federal government budget "pie."

I, for one, can't wait to see the look on my state senator's face when I show up with a few minivans full of pie-wielding PTA moms asking him to support allocating the equivalent of two percent of the more than $400 billion annually spent on defense for the purpose of creating a Department of Peace and Nonviolence. (See DOPcampaign.org for more info.)

Being more of a Rosanne than June Cleaver, my pie will come from Mrs. Smith via my grocery store freezer, but the desire for nonviolent solutions strikes at the heart of what it means to be a mother.

Whether it's a south side, ghetto mom watching her child gunned down in a senseless crack war or a country club, West Point mother being told that her kid was one of the ones who didn't make it back—there's not a mother alive who can ever wrap her mind around a rational need for her child to die.

When our ancestors first talked about a creating a government built around the concept of liberty, people thought they were crazy. But they took an idea they held in their hearts and created an infrastructure around it. It wasn't easy, but they did it. We mothers have held peace in our hearts for long enough. It's time to make it an official part of our government.

Looking at the history books, our past requests for peace seem to have been as futile as turning down the pages of a catalogue and leaving it on the back of the toilet. But times have changed, and I, for one, can't be placated with chocolate anymore. I want my kids to have more than a piece of peace in their lifetime. I want the whole Whitman's sampler.

Second-Guessing the Other Guy's Values is a Cheap Way Out

Have you ever noticed that whenever somebody says somebody else "doesn't share our values," they never mean it as a compliment?

Citing value differences is a socially acceptable way of saying, "Their primary basis of thinking obviously is immoral and ill-informed, so everything they come up with is completely flawed." The phrase, "They don't have the same values we do," usually is uttered with great disdain by pious people who are sure that their own values are the correct ones.

The "values" word gets big play during election years. Many of us find it impossible to believe the other side is operating with the same moral compass we are. If they knew the difference between right and wrong and believed in the future of this country the way we do, they'd never support that guy. Don't they know he's evil incarnate?

My mother was a political activist back in the 1970s, before value attacks had reached a fever pitch. One of her pet issues was the environment.

In one particularly memorable tree-hugging campaign, she rallied our entire community against local authorities trying to put in a huge highway. She dragged us kids along to meetings, rallies, and marches. We wore buttons, we lobbied, we passed out leaflets with pictures of the beaver pond. And, in the end, we lost. The highway went through, and the beavers were forced to find another home. But as a result of my mother's efforts, the state agreed to put in extensive parks and nature trails as part of the project.

And that's the way our political system is supposed to work.

Opposing groups have different ideas, and the fight between the factions nets a better result than either group would have come up with alone. Those "progress at any price" politicians would have plowed right through our neighborhood if my mother hadn't rallied the community to protect our environment. And many commuters would be snaking their way through residential areas if the highway had been stopped.

Our two-party political system evolved out of different approaches to problems and different views of what constitutes advancement. The problem now is we don't argue about the solutions—we argue about the candidates. Who did what when, what church do they go to, and, by all means, let's get a list of everybody they've slept with.

I may have selective memory, but I can't ever recall anybody asking my mother about her sex life when she was handing out petitions. It might have made for an interesting debate. Who wants to hear about beavers and traffic patterns when we could be talking about sex or religion?

Picking apart another person's perceived flaws is more satisfying to the ego than analyzing a problem. It appeals to our lowest instincts. If somebody's ideas rub us the wrong way, attacking the moral basis for their thinking gives us an easy out for not even considering the validity of their arguments. That's why the "paint your opponent as an evil, lying scum bucket" strategy is so effective.

When my mom chained herself to the tree, people knew what was important to her. They didn't have to dig around in her past to figure out what she was all about. Her lifetime of service spoke for itself.

You can't judge a person's values based on what their opponent says about them in a thirty-second smear commercial. The only way you can truly understand someone's values is to take a close look at what they say and do. Look at where they've invested their time and energy over the course of their lives. And listen to the details when they talk about their plans for the future.

It's been over five years since the tragedies of September 11, and if there ever was a time when we needed real leaders, it's now. Sound bites didn't get us into this mess and sound bites won't get us out of it.

The negative campaigners may encourage snap judgments about moral values based on differences in policy ideas. But if you value your voice in this country, you won't fall for it.

15

Are Corporate Witches Getting a Bum Rap?

"I ran the wrong kind of business,
but I did it with integrity."

—SYDNEY BIDDLE BARROWS,
THE "MAYFLOWER MADAM"

Riding High on a Pink Broomstick

Demanding. Tough. Aggressive. Apply these words to a man, and it's a compliment. Say the same things about a woman, and it's not quite so flattering. Any woman who's spent time in the business world knows all too well about the double bind that requires us to act like men in order to get ahead and then penalizes us for being unfeminine when we do.

A woman who speaks her mind and takes charge is labeled a witch with a capital *B*. A guy who does the same thing usually gets promoted.

The bizarre rules of corporate America are rooted in a leadership model core to the nature of men. The unspoken male pecking order decides who gets to shout the orders and who's supposed to shut up and take them.

Women never totally fit in because the male hierarchical approach was wired into men's genetic coding shortly after the dawn of time. When you're tracking a beast or ambushing an opponent, a command-and-control leadership model gets the job done. If you're going to arm guys with spears, the last thing you need is for them is to start voicing their own opinions.

Mother Nature wired women for a different approach. When you find yourself alone with a pack of screaming cave kids, a fire that needs stoking, and a food supply dependent upon a bag of seeds in your loincloth, collaborative methods are the only way you're going to get anything done.

It's no coincidence that men took their previously successful organizational models into the modern workplace. With brains that process information one chunk at a time, a "biggest guy wins" structure is the most effective way for them to function. And with surges of testosterone coursing through their veins, ruthless competition in the workplace may be the only thing that keeps men from killing each other. Dueling laser pointers and Blackberries are safer weapons than bows and arrows.

But had women been in charge of the workplace from the get-go, husbands would not be allowed to take paternity leave—they would be required to. Self-expression would be encouraged, company restrooms would stock free tampons, and cover-up sticks in shades ranging from ebony to alabaster would be an office expense just like coffee.

But the biggest difference would be in the way businesses are organized. Instead of being structured around who's in charge of who, organizations would be arranged around the actual work to be done. Just like a well-run PTA, companies would operate as an ever-moving network of committees. Well-respected, peer-chosen leaders would ask people how they wanted to contribute, and assignments would be made accordingly. Rewards would be based on contributions, not senior management face time. And everybody would get misty-eyed at the end of a job well done.

Women have made some significant changes in the world of work. Lifetime Television actually does stock tampons and hair spray in its ladies rooms. And the Fortune 500 currently has ten—count 'em, ten—women CEOs. But for every woman who made it to the top, hundreds of wanna-be leaders are wasting away in middle-management mediocrity, walking zombies who tried to act like men and lost their sense of self in the process.

Ladies, it's time to let the men be men. They're the only ones who are really good at it, and if their way works for them, let them have at it. Communication and commitment are a woman's forte, and when we apply our feminine wiles to the workplace we create our own environment for success.

A more cynical woman might point out the ability to track large game has very little marketability these days, whereas influencing others is a skill that has withstood the test of time.

But instead, I'll just ask you to think about Enron and Mary Kay. Which group of hotshot flashy boys are out of business and whose "work part time, having fun with your girlfriends" company is going strong even after her death?

Mary Kay Ash was demanding, tough, aggressive—and a very nice woman. Her multimillion-dollar business is proof the chick way works. And if corporate America doesn't support it, feel free to take your talents elsewhere.

You don't have to trade in your car for a broomstick to be successful. Real women act like themselves and drive their Pink Caddy all the way to the bank.

Casualties of the Mommy Wars

The bell rings, and round three of the mommy wars begins.

As the battle of cubicles heats up, the moms face off. It's the parents vs. the non-parents, and it's a fight to the death. The prize? The right to a private life.

The winner gets to waltz out at 4:55 p.m., and the loser has to stay shackled to their desk for the rest of the night.

In the ever-raging "My life choices are better than yours" brawl, the competitors have changed. It used to be the stay-at-home moms vs. the working moms, but the latest skirmish is between the women in the office who have children and those who don't.

In the Cheerios corner is the frazzled working mother. Guilt is her mantra, and she's desperate to pick up little Suzie by six because day care charges a dollar a minute if you're late. In the Cosmo corner is her childless counterpart. Sure, she may be spending her evenings eating sushi in front of the TV, or, gasp, even on a date, but does that make her leisure time any less valuable?

I've been both a combatant and a casualty of this war. I supported the mom side with my comments in the *O Magazine* article, "The Mother of All Conflicts," but I well remember what it was like on the other end.

Pre-kids, I thought: "Look, you decided to have children, so you need to deal with it on your own time. Just because Junior has his twelfth ear infection of the season doesn't mean it's my job to pick up your slack."

I wanted to be nice, but other people's kids were their problem, and I didn't think a school play should be the winning trump card in deciding who gets to opt out of that nasty trip to Toledo.

But that was before I gave birth to the future president of the United States.

Now that I'm a mom, I'm knee-deep in the struggle between wanting to do a great job at work and wanting to be a good mom at home. Part of me wants to scream: "I'm raising the people who are going to create world peace and pay your social security, so the rest of you num-nuts better help me out or we're all doomed!" But when a kid commitment forces me to abandon my job, another part of me wants to slink out with a Post-it stuck to my forehead that reads: mother = half-baked contributor.

However, what I find even more disturbing than all the anxiety around this issue is the fact that we women are turning it on each other.

New York Times columnist Lisa Belkin suggests, "The battle strikes at the heart of what it means, traditionally, to be a woman." At the root of the conflict is the need for validation. Belkin says: "On both sides, women hear judgment. On both sides, they want their lives affirmed."

For every childless woman pulling double duty at the office, there's a working mom going home to bed and baths, and then putting in a third shift cranking out work she couldn't get to during the day. Beating up on each other may provide an outlet for our anger and stress, but it masks the real problem, which is that we're all working all the time.

Instead of sparring with our peers, maybe it's time to take

the gloves off and slap some sense into the organizations perpetuating this mess.

Heavyweight champs may tough it out for twelve rounds, but this is one bout where the last one in the ring doesn't get any prize at all.

Is Your Ratty Bathrobe the New Power Suit?

Whether it's an urban myth or a practical reality, many people believe you can't be a good mother and knock back a six-figure income at the same time.

The truth is, of course you can. Women do it all the time. Though having been down that road myself, I found the loss of sleep, lack of personal time, and a marriage that was starting to resemble an exhausted tag-team wrestling duo were too heavy prices to pay. For a generation raised to believe you can "bring home the bacon, fry it up in the pan, and never let him forget he's the man," it's a bit of a shock to discover that a baby doesn't always fit inside your briefcase.

But can you devote your days solely to your kids and still feel like a fabulous human being in your own right? I'm always envious of those who do it well, but many of us find it a struggle to keep our sense of self while we're scrubbing the toilets and passing out PB&Js.

The problem isn't work vs. family—it's our either/or way of thinking and the system that created it. The reality is, if you want to meet the school bus every day, it's highly unlikely that a major corporation is going to pay you big bucks to do it.

But there's a difference between big jobs and big money. Big jobs are what somebody else pays you to do. The kind of job where your employer owns your time and when they say jump, the only acceptable answer is "how high?"

Big money, however, is something you can make on your own. The trouble is, many of us don't believe it's possible to do it. We think if we want to be good mothers, we have to piddle along in low-pay, part-time jobs or give up working altogether.

There's nothing wrong with staying home or working in a lower paying job you love. Yet I wonder how many women-owned businesses stay small simply because we think being super-successful and being a hands-on mom are two mutually exclusive objectives.

It's almost like we have a mental block that says, "Women who make six figures aren't good mothers." Perhaps that's because many men in that income bracket have typically made huge personal sacrifices to get there. But it doesn't have to be that way.

The corporate world is based on the model men knew best: Single-mindedly focus on the hunt, compartmentalize your family into something you do when you get home, and keep your spear sharp, or we'll all get killed.

Dragging a bunch of kids along or taking time to breast-feed only slows things down. And heaven forbid if you should get engrossed in a personal conversation. The big beast gets away faster than you can describe what's on sale at TJ Maxx.

Women, however, operate with a totally different mentality: Handle six things at once, integrate work with family, chat with your girlfriends to keep your energy up, and use your creativity to get it all done on time.

The secret of making big money, for men or women, is working in an environment that suits you. For many women that means working alongside your pals and being in a job that pays you based on results—not how many nights you stay late at the office. As necessity is the mother of invention, mothers are the inventors of the home party business. What's not to love? Get a few girls together, buy some cool new stuff, make a little money, and be home in time to tuck the kids into bed.

But as much as I admire Mary Kay and the visionary business model she created, I always assumed the gals working the chick party circuit weren't making much dough. Imagine my shock when I discovered that many of these ladies are knocking back major cash.

Intimacy expert Patty Brisben, the founder and CEO of Pure Romance (www.PureRomance.com) says, "Our top consultant made over six figures hosting only a couple parties a week and was still able to attend her children's basketball, baseball, and football games, and accompany her daughter touring the state in horse-riding competitions."

Six figures for going to a few parties and selling "romance and relationship enhancement products" to your girlfriends part-time? And I thought being a writer was a cushy gig. If we ever wanted economic proof the chick way works, this is it.

Net worth doesn't have to equal self worth, but it's not an inverse relationship either.

February may be the official "National Doing Business in Your Bathrobe Month," according to www.WebMomz.com, but those of us who traded in our pantyhose for pink bunny slippers celebrate it every day.

Moms who create their own work environment bring home big bags of bacon and keep themselves in their kid's lives at the same time. It's up to you whether you fry it up in a pan, but remember, being a six-figure earner will never make you a man.

16

Is Your Brain Ruining Your Life?

"The brain is a wonderful organ. It starts working the moment you get up in the morning and does not stop until you get into the office."

—ROBERT FROST

Looking for a Common Denominator?
"The common denominator in all your failed relationships is YOU!"

My sister and I found this truism on a "demotivational" poster on www.Despair.com, a site that offers a hilarious "bleak perspective" on the ever-cheery corporate posters, calendars, and coffee mugs.

Call me a cynic, but I've always been skeptical of those rah-rah motivational messages. A crew of sweaty guys rowing does not inspire me to greater heights of company teamwork.

My sister and I got a big laugh over the common denominator poster and then went back to work, secure in the knowledge that it didn't apply to us. Two weeks later I was on the road in Florida, touring for my book, *Forget Perfect*. Before you start thinking paparazzi and glamour, let me clarify the details. It was my first book, and while John Grisham gets an escort and limo, I, on the other hand, was navigating the roads of Tampa alone in a tiny rental car.

After finding myself lost and late for the third time in three days, I started to lose it. I had gotten directions from three different TV stations, and they were all bad. As I called a friend and began ranting and raving about how nobody knows how to give good directions, I suddenly realized—Oh my God, it's ME! The poster was right. Three different sets of directions from three different people, and the one who got lost every time was me.

Connecting my current navigational problems to a few other areas of my life, I began to see a common trend in my annoyances with others. A random polling of friends reveals I'm not alone. We've all got our own particular hot buttons. The players may change, but we often find ourselves in eerily similar situations over and over again. And the frustrations we have with others can reveal more about our own personal neuroses than about theirs.

Somebody who's always complaining about people being so controlling? I hate to break it to you, but if this is your beef, you're letting people control you. You might not be walking around with a big sign that says, "Make my decisions for me," but you're giving out the vibe that your opinion doesn't count much. It's a convenient way to get out of standing up for yourself, but it's a pretty stifling gig over the long haul of your life.

On the opposite end is the "Do I always have to be in charge of everything?" syndrome. The answer is—yes, you do. Until you give yourself permission to step aside, very few will dare to challenge your authority. That feeling of discomfort when nobody steps up to the plate or even notices what needs to be done? That emotion is entirely yours.

Another common peeve is, "This group is so cliquish," often uttered by the person standing on the sidelines, waiting for others to invite them in. When you interpret people's delight in each other's company as a plot to keep you out, the only big loser is you.

Most of our beefs with the universe stem from the fact that everybody forgot to read the "memo on the world, according to me." Your best chance at true happiness is overcoming your own biases and learning to enjoy the people around you, warts and all.

We're all the star of our own movie, and while we may be the common denominator when it goes wrong, we can also be the common denominator when it goes right.

Making Your Marriage Miserable in Your Mind? Maybe.
What's the biggest blocker to intimacy in your relationship?

Is it your husband's stubborn refusal to open up? Your wife's bizarre notion that dusting the top of the TV is more important than sex? Or perhaps it's meddling in-laws, clingy kids, and demanding bosses who have a stranglehold on you and your spouse?

For most of us, it's none of the above.

As delightful as it would be to reprogram everybody else, the biggest barrier to intimacy is usually smack in the middle of our own brains. Imagine my shock when I dove into *The Complete Idiot's Guide to Intimacy* with my yellow highlighter in hand, ready to mark pertinent passages for my husband, only to discover I was the one who "had issues."

I must have been the exact idiot author Dr. Paul Coleman had in mind when he wrote about "your inner announcer calling the play-by-play."

Coleman (Paul-Coleman.com) cites the "self-serving inner dialogue that builds a case against your partner" as the reason why you can spend your drive home ruminating about past and current relationship conflicts and arrive at your doorstep feeling like you already had a fight.

An argument with your spouse when he's not even there? Guess who wins that one.

Coleman effectively illustrates what most of us already know and prefer to ignore—"Your mind, unleashed at even a fraction of its potential, can create your own heaven or hell."

I've often said that every relationship has three dimensions: the one in your head, the one in your partner's head, and the one that everybody else would see if Nora Ephron made it into a movie. But what's not quite as obvious is how the part in one person's brain affects the other two. As a long-time student of human behavior, I've observed first-hand what countless studies prove: Nonverbal communication is more powerful than speaking, and tone of voice has more impact than the words themselves.

The verbiage coming out of your mouth might be, "Anything you say, dear." But if your actual thoughts are more along the lines of, "Here we go again, another round of your negative, asinine behavior, Mr. Mountain of Toenail Clippings On My Good Couch," that's the message your partner's going to take away.

You might think you're being as nice as you can with that sugar-sweet voice, but as any shrink or talk show host will tell you, your thoughts are being revealed by your tone and body language whether you like it or not.

And if your brain interprets your spouse's every look as a glare and views his or her every action through the filter of "here comes that evil witch again," you're hardly on the road to a more intimate relationship.

Coleman identifies four pathways to greater intimacy with the one you love: thought, talk, touch, and togetherness. We may believe that lacking talk, touch, or togetherness is the root of all our problems, but Coleman eloquently makes the case that our thoughts are always the precursor to the other three. Women usually want more talk, while men often complain that there's not enough touch. And overworked, stressed-out couples everywhere know that when togetherness constantly takes such a backseat to kids and jobs, nobody's happy.

But how many of us consider the mental track in our own minds when we're craving a closer connection? Yes, men would be better off learning to share more feelings. And, yes, women need to accept that a husband's desire for sex is often his way of expressing his heartfelt love. And, of course, scheduling time together is critical to any long-term commitment.

Yet how we respond to our partner's requests for talk, touch, or togetherness all depends on our own frame of mind at the time. Our internal dialogue creates the environment our spouse's actions have to enter.

A friend of mine, whose husband travels frequently, told me, "Home alone with the kids, I continually found myself frustrated with him for being gone, and then I suddenly realized—I'm creating a bad marriage in my own mind."

Imagine her clueless, hard-working hubby eagerly coming home to a wife who'd spent three days stewing about his faults. The scene would be pathetically laughable if so many other husbands across America—including mine—weren't experiencing the same thing.

Thought, talk, touch, and togetherness require time and effort from both sides, but changing your internal dialogue is something you can do on your way home from work this week.

Intimacy—it's all in your head. Now there's a thought.

Half-Brained Workers Have a Competitive Advantage

Do you ever forget to take your brain to work? Or maybe you've got one of those jobs that only takes half your brain to do it.

I still shudder at the memory of the smoke-infested summer I spent in a darkened cocktail lounge serving over-priced bourbon and waters. As I counted down the hours every night until 2 a.m., my mind wandered between cursing my evil boss for making us wear high heels and calculating how much more money I still needed for next year's tuition.

I'm also embarrassed to admit how many hours I've clocked on my "mom job" without being fully present. My body was serving chicken nuggets, but my mind was somewhere else altogether. However, while some might accuse the daydreamers amongst us of being less than focused on the tasks at hand, to say that we're making a half-brained effort would actually be a compliment.

It turns out most of us aren't even cracking fifty percent.

Best-selling author and meditation teacher John Selby (JohnSelby.com) says, "Most people are operating at twenty to twenty-five percent awareness." That means seventy-five percent of your thoughts are not about what you're doing at the moment. And in a work situation, it's often even worse.

Referring to what he calls the "awareness or attentive variable," Selby suggests that, "At any given moment, an employee can be at ten to twenty percent awareness." Thank gawd I wasn't only getting ten to twenty percent of my paycheck.

Your awareness is basically what your mind chooses to consciously pay attention to, or, more accurately, where you consciously choose to direct it.

Selby, author of *Take Charge of Your Mind: Core Skills to Enhance Your Performance, Well Being and Integrity at Work*, says, "The people who succeed at work best are those who succeed in focusing in the present moment."

MBA programs may teach the art of strategic planning and business analysis, but worrying about the future and ruminating about the past won't improve your current performance one iota. It doesn't matter whether you're managing or mommying, the only way to be really good at it is to keep a big chunk of your brain in the present moment.

As someone who has made a good bit of her living teaching people how to sell everything from widgets to waffle irons, I observed firsthand what a difference the awareness factor can make in someone's performance.

As part of a consulting project, I recently shadowed a group of biotech sales people. After days of watching them butter up receptionists, hand out free pens, and chase doctors down the hall, I realized there's something distinctly different going on inside the minds of top performers. The best people aren't thinking more thoughts at work; they're actually thinking less.

The average distracted Joe or Jane has multiple thought tracks running through his or her head all the time. "Did I remember to bring the right handout?" "I wonder if our health insurance will cover my wart removal?" "Did I forget to turn the stove off?" "I think cute, little Alex in accounting was giving me the eye this morning."

But high-performing people have no such filters; they're totally focused on the person in front of them and the task at hand.

So the good news is if you want to get better at your job—or anything else you're applying your time and talents to—you don't have to work any harder. All you have to do is flip the switch in your head to "on," or at least bump up the wattage a bit.

Of course, you'll probably never get yourself up to a hundred percent, but even a half-lit bulb will outshine the rest of us dim wits.

17

Why Does Mom Always Hold the Barf Bucket?

"Motherhood has a very humanizing effect.
Everything gets reduced to essentials."

—MERYL STREEP

Are Girlfriends the Mojo of Marriage?

A friend of mine is going back to work after her first baby, and like most first-time moms, she has everything planned to perfection.

Armed with a flow chart and a calculator, she's crafted a master plan whereby she will work the late shift, her husband will work early, and their darling child will never be placed in the arms of anyone but her loving parents.

She's a TV news producer who will be busy cranking out compelling stories about murder and death from 4 p.m. to midnight. And hubby is a first-shift paramedic who will only save lives between 7 a.m. and 3 p.m. once his wife goes back to work.

As a woman who's well acquainted with the overly ambitious "the baby will be well-cared for, but we'll never see each other again" routine, all I could tell her was, "Be careful." As she described their daunting schedule, I noticed two big things missing: time as a couple and time with her friends.

"Oh, no, no," she assured me, "We'll be together as a family all weekend, and I work with my friends."

Sorry, sugar—it ain't the same.

Having once spent an entire year of my life without husband or girlfriend time, I didn't have the heart to tell her that by denying her husband time alone with her and denying herself time with her friends, she was literally sucking the life out of her marriage.

It's a funny thing—a man may be the most committed father on the planet, but if he doesn't get some good wife time every week, his energy starts to wane. And a woman may love her hubby and kids to death, but a lack of girlfriend time will make her slowly go insane.

It's like the man gets his energy from the woman, and the women gets her energy from her friends. And when either party can't dip their toes in the appropriate mojo fountain often enough, the entire system runs dry no matter how many Diet Cokes and triple lattes you chug down.

A guy may have tons of buddies, but for most men their best friend—their emotional touchstone—is usually their wife. My own husband says, "Men need male friends, but it's being alone with your wife that really revives you." I hate to disillusion the poker night crew, but wifely attention beats a straight flush every time.

Family time may feel like togetherness to a woman, but for a man to feel truly rejuvenated, the time has to be one-on-one with his wife. I'm not talking just about sex, though most men earnestly tout the therapeutic value of time in the sack. I'm talking about the circle of energy in a family.

And it usually starts with the wife, which is why she needs to turn outside her relationship to fuel up. You may be married to Prince Charming, but there's nothing like a night out with the other village maidens to keep you from feeling like the palace wench. It's not just because margaritas taste better when you don't have to make them yourself. There's actually sound scientific evidence that confirms why female friends are essential to a woman's mental health.

A study from the UCLA medical school a few years back indicated that when women are with their women friends their brains release a feel-good hormone called oxytocin that cascades all the way through their bodies and does what Prozac and Percocet can't touch.

That's why a woman can come back from a night out with her gal pals and literally feel like a new person. (It's more likely she's feeling like her old self—the one who hadn't been sucked dry by everybody else.)

There are three important activities that can trigger an oxytocin release in women: childbirth, breast feeding, and being with other women. As much as I enjoyed breast-feeding and childbirth, they're not really hobbies I'd like to continue in my forties.

But ironically enough, as my returning-to-work friend is quickly discovering, childbirth and breast-feeding are the precise things that can bring that energy-restoring girlfriend time to a screeching halt. And as every man knows, if mom's feeling guilty for not spending enough time with Suzy and Sammy, an evening spent fawning over him is the last thing on her list.

Such is the double bind of parenthood. All the energy gets directed to the kids, and mom and dad are so sapped they don't schedule the activities that would fuel them up.

I think I'd better call my perfectly scheduled producer friend back. She's missing a few items on that flow chart, and I suggest she writes these two in ink.

A Tale of Two Vacations

It was the best of times, it was the worst of the times.

I had the most fabulous vacation of my life. But the woman holding the sunscreen-slicked up baby on her hip, wading out to grab her chin-deep toddler before he fell into the deep end of the splash pool, didn't seem to be having a very good time at all. And judging from the evil glare she gave her husband who was cluelessly downing Red Stripes at the swim up bar, his fun was about to end as well.

Same resort, same sun, and same pineapple-skewered Bahama Mama margaritas, but two totally different vacations.

While my husband, my two kids, and I enjoyed moon-lit walks on the beach, romping in the surf, and hours on the chaise lounge reading back issues of *People,* while sipping watered down daquiris, I watched other families struggle with hats that wouldn't stay on, try to yank floaties onto chubby sunburned arms, and deal with screaming fits in the middle of restaurants.

When we were cheerfully chomping down at the all-you-can-eat crab claw buffet, the cranky moms and dads were searching for the Sponge Bob sippy cup underneath the table.

Why did we have a great time while other families looked downright miserable? Is it because we're smarter or better looking? Or perhaps we're more spiritually enlightened and organized?

No, we had more fun simply because we're older. Or more precisely, our kids are older.

After years of stressful "I can't believe we paid money for this" vacations, I have finally discovered the secret of a fabulous family getaway: Do not take any children under the age of six. I like little kids, I really do. I even had two of them myself. But after years of dragging them to beaches and amusements parks in search of fun, I now realize that it's practically impossible to enjoy a vacation when you travel with someone who can't carry their own luggage.

I'm not quite sure when or how it happened, but finally at ages eight and thirteen, my two daughters can pack for themselves, put on their own sunscreen and get this—wake up quietly and go down to the breakfast buffet without mom or dad. Sure, they had OD'd on Fruit-Loops by the time we showed up, but that extra hour of sleep made it feel like a real vacation.

No more schlepping around a yellow plastic diaper bag, no more fumbling with car seat straps, no more sleeping perched over a rickety port-a-crib, and best of all, no more fighting about who's supposed to be watching the kids.

From my chaise lounge vantage point this week, I couldn't help but notice how many couples spent a good bit of their vacation annoyed with each other. Or more accurately, how many men had to suffer the wrath of a wife unaided. Time and time again I watched as the male member of the tag team awkwardly waited on the sidelines for a wifely request that, unbeknownst to him, was already being communicated via weary sighs, darting glares, and endless eye rolling.

The women were exhausted from non-stop duty as life-guard, snack patrol, nap monitor, and overall cruise director, and the poor men were wondering when the fun was going to start.

If I hadn't lived it myself so many times, it might be funny.

In hindsight, I wish I hadn't been so hard on my husband during those years. I also wish I'd incorporated more child care into the mix, whether it meant taking along a teenage sitter, inviting my parents, or spending the big bucks for a resort with a kiddie club.

So if you've got older kids, join me at the Pina Colada dispenser; you've earned a break. But if you've got little ones, and you're still expecting everyone to have fun when you travel, you're vacationing in a fool's paradise.

18

Does Santa-Claus Get Anxiety Attacks?

"Is it a hallmark moment,
or the worst week of your life?"

—RICHARD CARLSON
(DON'T GET SCROOGED)

Thanks for the Misery

The holidays might be over, but the lingering effect of time spent with extended family can make you feel like a boxer who just spent twelve rounds up against the ropes.

Whether you spent the holidays tossing and turning on your sister-in-law's flimsy sofa bed with a metal cross brace jamming into your back or trying to explain to your rosary-clutching mother-in-law that your kids really are Jewish—conflicts with the in-laws can have a chilling effect on a marriage.

Your family does it one way, your spouse's family does it another, and when the two cultures come together under one roof, tempers flare faster than a fuse box overloaded with forty-seven strands of lights. If you came out of the dueling, candy cane war this year unscathed, consider yourself lucky. For many people, a holiday with the in-laws is an event to be endured, not enjoyed.

A friend of mine spent last Christmas vacation on twenty-four hour peanut patrol. She was amazed to discover that after going to great lengths to arrange a peanut-free flight for her highly allergic toddler, she entered her in-laws' home to find them making peanut butter buckeyes at the kitchen table. Although they'd been told exposure to nuts was extremely dangerous for the child, the women in the family continued their long-standing tradition of bringing out peanut-laden goodies all week long. While it might be tempting to write off her in-laws as a barrel of mixed nuts, I doubt they're the first family so determined to do things their way that they make life miserable for anyone who has the audacity to marry in.

If there's one relationship that ignites angst over conflicting traditions more than any other, it has to be the one between mother-in-law and daughter-in-law. Many women may struggle to please their own mothers, but I doubt there's a woman alive who does things exactly the way her mother-in-law thinks she should. And since women typically own the holidays, when the wreaths go up, the gloves go on. While the men are slugging back the eggnog in front of the tube, the women are in the kitchen seething because some interloping in-law had the audacity to sprinkle powdered sugar over Grandma's prized fruitcake.

There's a reason why a meddling or overly critical mother-in-law is always good for a few laughs on a TV sitcom—everyone either knows or has one.

There's nothing like watching her son's wife do something

differently to bring out the beast in a woman. It doesn't matter if the issue is opening two presents instead of one on Christmas Eve or whether on not Junior gets to play with his dreidle during services, problems ensue when the daughter-in-law doesn't do it the way the mom did. The mother-in-law feels invalidated, the daughter-in-law feels judged, and the poor husband/son is in the middle, feeling like the two women in his life have his head in a vise.

However, unless the guy wants to die a painful, lingering death, there's only one way out: jump onto his wife's side as fast as he possibly can.

In my friend's case, her husband stood up to his mother and said that for the safety of his child, they were going to have to go buckeye-free during the holidays or he and his family would not be back. Other marriage moments might not be quite as dramatic, but in the end a smart man will always side with his wife.

The mother-in-law may determine how long the sparring goes on, but in the battle for family traditions, the last woman standing is usually the younger one. Wise mothers-in-law retire gracefully and never step foot into the ring. And smart daughters-in-law pick their battles carefully.

Now back to your corners, ladies. The rematch starts November 1.

Sloppy Entertaining: The Latest Rage in Holiday Parties
Strap on your engines. A new season of America's roughest, nastiest, full-contact, competitive sport has begun. That's right, it's time for holiday entertaining.

We all know what the perfect party looks like. A designer-clad hostess serves elegant hors d'oeuvres in her immaculately clean, fabulously decorated, showplace house—sans any evidence of dirty socks or pet hair, of course—without ever chipping a nail. Meanwhile, her guests are oohing and ahhing over the hand-monogrammed fingerbowls thinking, "I could never invite her over to my house—I sure wouldn't want her see the way we live!"

Entertaining is supposed to be fun, but we often put so much pressure on ourselves we don't feel like we can have anybody over unless things are absolutely perfect. The result: We don't entertain very often, and when we do it's more work than fun. Whether it's trying to impress our husband's coworkers, pretending we're perfect for the church crowd, or proving to our in-laws that we're fully capable of hosting a holiday meal, many of us feel like our womanhood is on the line every time we have somebody over.

I've got big news for you: The only one measuring you and your house against those TV and magazine standards is you. Most of us are so happy to get invited anywhere, you could feed us Chex Mix with convenience store eggnog, and we wouldn't care.

I learned this little lesson the hard way. I used to give one of those over-the-top parties. For the first fifteen years of my marriage, I spent most of December cooking, cleaning and decorating, all in anticipation of my big blowout on Dec. 23rd, when a hundred of my family and friends were treated to the "best" holiday party ever. My house was spit-shined to a high gloss, and there were lit candles as far the eye could see. Of course, I had to make my kids live on the porch for a few days to create that ambience. But what the heck, it made it easier to clean up the fast food trash every night. December was no time for real cooking; I spent my evenings piping lemon cream cheese into little pastry crusts. Sure it was a big sacrifice, but I was a "hostest with the mostest," and nobody gave a better party than I.

I always assumed my fab parties endeared me to my friends. But I did wonder why so few ever returned my hospitality. I finally figured it out when one of my husband's colleagues said, "We've always wanted to invite you back, but I could never give a party like that." Here I had been busting my buns, and these poor people went home worried they couldn't measure up.

Perfect parties don't make people like you more; they just make them feel intimidated.

Martha Stewart, God love her tenacious soul, even works on Christmas (except when she's in jail). I'll save you the passé jokes about prison turkey, but I will remind you her job was to invite viewers in for visually appealing TV, not relaxed conversations to deepen their relationships.

I hope you'll do some entertaining this holiday season. We all deserve more time with our friends. But I also hope you don't make yourself crazy in the process.

Be the first in your crowd to try these five tips for Sloppy Entertaining, and the rest of us real women will love you forever:

1. **THINK PLASTIC.** Save the fine china for when the queen visits. Buy themed paper products—nobody gives a hoot. Add a 55-gallon Hefty bag for cleanup, and you're good to go.

2. **WEAR ELASTIC.** Lose the body-squeezing undergarment. You deserve permission to exhale. Buy yourself a fab blouse, drape it over basic black with an elastic waistband, and join us at the bean dip.

3. **BUY IN BULK.** Forgo fancy canapés, save your sanity,

and load up on prepackaged food at the warehouse club, or even slip in some takeout. Your mother-in-law will never know, and your girlfriends will never tell.

4. **DELEGATE DRUDGERY.** Hostess doesn't mean "hand servant." If you want a weekend job waiting tables, there are plenty of places you can get one. Ask people to bring stuff, and put kids, husbands, and relatives to work. If the crackers aren't artfully arranged in a fan-shaped pattern, nobody but you will care.

5. **DITCH THE DAZZLING DECOR.** Forget the trappings and trimmings, and focus on family and friends, and have some fun. Sure, it's less work, but let's face it, you're worth it.

Making Holiday Magic Happen Causes Nothing but Grief.

Webster's New World Dictionary defines *holiday* as "a day of freedom from labor."

Holiday may mean a day of rest, but *The Holidays* refer to a month of non-stop work for women. If you're not insane by mid December, you're taking way too much Percocet.

It doesn't matter if you're a truck driver or TV executive; if you're a woman, you still own the holiday to-do list. And if your kids are going to have matching sweaters this season, you better get out and buy them.

Children joyfully count down the days on the Advent calendar, and husbands wonder if the jewelry store still serves free martinis on Christmas Eve, but most of the women I know suffer heart palpitations worrying how they'll get it all done. The rest of the family goes to sleep with visions of sugarplums dancing in their heads, but the female half of the species is tossing and turning all night, wondering what she's going to buy her husband's Aunt Vera.

Having a baby in a manger with no epidural would be a vacation compared to what most women put themselves through during the holidays. Christmas is supposed to be the celebration of a birth, but for many of us, it feels like a slow, grinding death. In fact, the process is a bit like the five stages of grief.

DENIAL: This year it will be different. I'll get the cards in the mail over Thanksgiving. My husband will help with the decorating. I'll buy all my gifts online in time for early shipping, and baking will be fun because the kids are going to help.

ANGER: Since when I am responsible for everybody else's Christmas? Half these people don't even send us a card back, and if my husband doesn't get off the couch to help put up this tree, I'm going to scream. I can't believe those bloody PTA moms had the nerve to ask me to send in "three home-baked pies" for the teachers. Don't these women have anything else to do? I hope nobody expects me to clean up all this glitter.

DEPRESSION: This holiday has lost all meaning—I don't know why I even bother. I bet he doesn't even know what we're getting his mother. What have I done to make my children so greedy? I've probably put on ten pounds already. Nobody in this family even asked me what I want.

BARGAINING: If I get the gifts bought by the 22nd, maybe I won't have to pay overnight shipping. I'll put some Slice 'N Bakes on a pretty dish, and it will look like I was baking. A personal phone call means more than a card to my real friends. If I stuff myself into a body-squeezing undergarment maybe I can still get into my black dress. I'll drink one glass of mineral water for every glass of Chardonnay.

ACCEPTANCE: I'm a tired, broke, fat woman who did the best she could. Maybe next year will be different.

Wouldn't it be nice if, just once, we could start the season with acceptance and work our way through to joy? After all, we're not dealing with a real death, only the death of our illusions.

It can be truly fun to send cards. It can be fun to give a party, and it can even be fun to buy presents. The individual activities themselves aren't a problem; it's the cumulative effect that turns our magical dreams into a nightmare. The key to enjoying the holidays is keeping the list short enough so you can actually enjoy each item on it.

Just because you did it last year or your mother did it every year, doesn't mean it has to be a tradition. Pick and choose what you want, and do different things in different years. Photo cards one year, baking the next, and if you're not in the mood to decorate a tree, buy a poster of one, and hang it in your foyer.

Who cares what a guy named Webster has to say? Define the holidays on your own terms and give yourself permission to enjoy them.

Dried Out Decorations Fan the Flames of the Faithful

The world's religions are coming together, or at least that's my hope. It's either that, or we're all going to kill each other off in the fight over whose faith is more divine.

The annual flap over which holiday gets top billing in the Kmart ad merely accentuates the absurdity of the age-old religious quagmire we humans continue to perpetuate. It's the belief that any talk or endorsement of your God some-how belittles mine.

In her *Newsweek* column, "Frankincense In Aisle Five!" Anna Quindlen sums it up beautifully saying, "O ye of little faith, who believe that somehow the birth of Christ is dependent upon recognition in a circular from OfficeMax!"

Aside from the obvious spiritual incongruence of fighting over whose holiday gets the best commercial endorsements, think about the dilemma this poses for the poor retailers— "Do I put Jesus on the end cap and just give the Kwanzaa stuff an aisle display?" "What if I run out of dreidels and matzo balls? Will people think I'm anti-Semitic?"

Imagine a modern-day Joseph trying to decide how to decorate his "Carpenter and Son" van for the holidays. "Should we stay true to our heritage and hang blue and silver lights off the hood? What about a green wreath wired to the front grill? Will Mrs. Obama still hire us to build that big kinara in her foyer?"

I have a mental image of Jesus putting his arm around his father's shoulder saying, "Dad, lighten up. They're only decorations."

Somehow, in the fight to decide whose God is more holy, sane voices like those of Jesus, Mohammed, and Buddha seem to be lacking. If those three ever got together, I doubt they'd waste their time arguing about whose photo got to grace the corporate credit card. But a quick listen to talk radio reveals that in the quest to claim religious exclusivity, the annual holiday controversy only serves to fan the flame.

It's rather interesting that winter holidays (and I use that term loosely here) ignite all this religious angst because many of our modern holiday traditions are actually rooted in pagan celebrations. Community celebrations that began as a way to provide some fun in the middle of a cold, dark winter. Think no electricity, and you'll understand why a festival of lights with roasted boar was appealing.

The "one God" take on the holidays didn't begin until fourth- and fifth-century church leaders recognized that no peasant in their right mind would give up a warm fire and a mug of grog for a cold church pew. So they carried their crosses to the rabble's bonfires and claimed the holidays in the name of their faith.

Seventeen centuries later, we're still fighting about it. The teachings of Jesus endure, yet humanity's need to revel in our own righteousness often overshadows the spirit of his message.

But things always get worse before they get better. So I'm hoping that events of late may help intelligent people embrace the idea that perhaps the world's religions can do more than just coexist. Perhaps our collective faiths are part of a larger story that's bigger than we ever even dreamed.

Much like the winter solstice helped the peasants with no power, our holidays are just like our faith—they're a light to guide us through a long, dark night. And I really don't think God cares which brand of battery we choose to keep it lit.

19

Do Dead Mothers Make Better Fathers?

"The older I get, the smarter my father seems to get."

—TIM RUSSERT

Suburban Husbands: Gorillas in our Midst

If a kid falls down in the woods, can a man hear it if a woman is present? Not if she's his wife.

Why is it that the same guy who can spot the model number on his neighbor's chainsaw from five hundred feet doesn't even notice when his kid is gnawing on poisonous tree bark right under his nose?

Women have long complained that men aren't as attentive to the kids as they are, and some have suggested that perhaps they're just not wired for it. Yet I have observed many a dad who does quite fine on his own but suddenly becomes inept the minute a woman, especially his wife, shows up on the scene. It's like they turn off their parenting eyes and ears whenever a female is present.

I was at the zoo recently and happened to catch an up close glance of the "I thought you were watching them" syndrome so common in modern men. My kids and I were exiting the gorilla habitat, and we walked past a dad watching his toddling child. The mother was sitting fifteen feet away, and she looked like an exhausted mom who desperately needed a moment to herself.

She occasionally glanced over, but it was clear that, by mutual agreement, dad was in charge, and she was taking a breather from her wiggling kid, who stood banging his hands against the big glass wall.

As the little one got wilder and wilder, every mom in the zoo could see exactly what was going to happen next: The toddler slipped off the bench and tumbled to the ground below. Before dad even realized his kid was down, mom sprinted over, scooped up the kid and gave the father the evil eye.

She probably would have marched herself and the baby right out of that zoo—but the gorillas aren't allowed to leave their cage.

That's right, this typical little male/female scenario didn't involve the humans watching from outside the glass—it was the gorillas within. And it proved once again that all the nagging in the world cannot rewire the male brain.

In *The Female Animal,* author Irene Elia observed that when a mother and father monkey are sitting together and the baby monkey cries, the father won't react. He acts as though he can't even hear the baby. But if the mother isn't around and the baby cries, he will get up and attend to the infant.

I'm sure the ape moms find this just as annoying as their human counterparts, but this maddening behavior is so obviously intuitive, I have to wonder if things will ever change. Are we women doomed to 24/7 child care forever? Or is evolution eventually going to work its magic on the minds of men?

I'm no Jane Goodall or Dian Fossey, but I think I can translate what Mama Gorilla was saying with all her grunts, snorts, and dirty looks: "The one time I ask you to watch your baby so I can get a break and you don't even notice when he falls off a ledge. I manage to carry him around all day every day while I dig grubs for your dinner, and you can't even watch him for five minutes. I can hear him crying from halfway across the compound, and you're sitting there staring at that stupid glass like you haven't heard a thing. I swear you care more about watching those silly humans than you do about your own kids. I'm beginning to wonder if you're trying to do a bad job just so I won't ask you again."

A scientist friend of mine once told me that organisms don't change until outside pressure forces them to. Any man will tell you there's plenty of pressure on them to change, but the evolution of a species doesn't happen overnight. It's not like we sprang from the swamps and started walking erect just because someone's mother thought it was a good idea. Evolution takes time, and when you compare most men's parenting skills to those of their fathers, they've made a bigger jump forward than a whale that learned to fly. Male apes and humans don't consciously turn off their parenting eyes and ears when a woman shows up. Give them credit for figuring out how to turn them on when she leaves.

If the mother gorilla had taken a real break and gone out for banana daiquiris with her girlfriends, dad would have known he was the solo man in charge and risen to the occasion.

The co-parenting concept was invented by the sex who evolved through collaborative work; tag team parenting is more genetically encoded in men. Left to their own devices, most men can blaze a decent trail through the parenting forest—as long as some woman doesn't make the mistake of hovering around trying to give them directions.

Mamma's Boys Learn Subtraction and Turn Out Worse

"You don't have to deserve your mother's love. You have to deserve your father's. He's more particular." Pulitzer Prize-winning poet Robert Frost hit the nail on the head when he described the difference between mothers and fathers.

Have you ever noticed it's always the mother pleading for the convicted killer's life on death row? "But he's really a good boy, your honor." We moms stand up for our kids no matter what, and it's our personal mission to make sure the world treats our darlings right. We may scream at them in private, but we'll defend our kids to the death if anybody suggests they're anything less than perfect.

Dads are another story. They have no problem telling Junior he's not measuring up. When my husband puts on his manly authoritative voice to tell our daughters, "There are no acceptable excuses for being late," I find myself wincing for fear that he has bruised their fragile little egos. I resent always having to play the heavy hand, but when he steps in to discipline, I find myself criticizing the way he does the job.

The mother and father roles weren't always so blurred. But back in the '70s, huge numbers of women donned our mini-man uniforms—female versions of blue pinstripes and red silk ties—to head off to work and learn to act like men. We naturally assumed that men would acquire our skills at home, specifically when it came to the kids. However, very few men ever morphed into mommies. We were stunned; we were angry, but then we realized: Aha, what they need is training! And thus began the utterly unsuccessful project I refer to as TTT DIM—Trying To Turn Dads Into Moms.

Oh, sure, some dads managed to take on the tasks of mothers, but their core belief about the job was completely flawed. They thought the children had to prove themselves worthy to the world, but we moms know the world is lucky the "flesh of our flesh" grace us with their presence.

When it became obvious the guys weren't going to become our partners the way we wanted them to, many of us settled for making Dad the Mommy Assistant instead. Mom is the expert on all things pertaining to the kids. Dad gets to help, but his opinion is not required. Kids need consistency, and his different way of doing things detracts from our well-thought out approach. But a dad's different style isn't a subtraction problem. It doesn't take away from the mom approach; it adds to it. And the sum total is more than the individual parts. Or, at least, that's the way it's supposed to work. I wonder how many marital conflicts could be avoided if we just let them do it their way. And I wonder how many dads would get more involved if they felt free to be themselves.

Knowing you have the unconditional love of your mother can give you the strength to go out into the world. Working to meet the high expectations of your father is how you know what to do when you get there.

A friend of mine used to work for a greeting card company that donated their old inventory to prisons, so the inmates could send cards to their loved ones. On Mother's Day it was always a struggle to make sure there were enough cards for every prisoner who wanted to send one. But in a telling social statement, on Father's Day, they literally could not give them away and cases of cards sat unopened year after year.

It takes more than unconditional love to create a self-sufficient human. That loving mom may plead with the judge to save her darling's life, but a good dad might have kept him from being there in the first place.

"Mamma's Boy" isn't an insult for no reason. Dads may not always use perfect, supportive communication skills, but a man who expects the best of his children is a gift indeed.

I'm forever grateful to my own dad, Jay Earle, a man who went way beyond being a junior mommy.

Kill Off the Mom for Sitcom Success

Have you ever noticed how many sitcoms and movies start with the "Mom is dead, so watch how we all cope" plot line?

Whether it's the hysterical hijinks as Dad puts the reds in with the whites and adds too much soap or the touching moment when he has to handle an emotional issue without a woman there to help, "The Family With No Mom" seems tailor-made for TV or the big screen.

Thanks to TIVO, my kids have tortured me with endless reruns of *Full House*. There are nine full seasons of Danny Tanner and the gang coping with raising three girls alone. Yet the producers of *8 Simple Rules for Dating My Daughter* debated whether or not they could even continue the show after John Ritter died. Would the obstacles facing Ritter's TV wife be entertaining enough to hold our interest?

Dad going it alone can be touching and funny. A mom alone is often sad and boring. A missing-in-action dad might make good fodder for a Lifetime movie where mom has to tackle the world by her lonesome. However, a missing mother provides enough humor and emotion for endless rounds of syndication. The only thing you can't eke out of a dead mother scenario is an action movie.

Interesting TV and film is based on emotional interactions. Watching a guy try to connect with the people around him or learn to handle mundane tasks can be uplifting. Whether it's Andy Griffith doing a great job raising Opie, Dennis Quaid dealing with preteen angst in *The Parent Trap*, or Mel Gibson finally understanding *What Women Want*— nothing is more appealing than watching a guy grow.

To create compelling scenarios you have to put a person in uncomfortable circumstances, and unfortunately for men, that's often interacting with their families. Women have learned to adopt a lot of the typical male roles, but for some reason many men are more removed from family life than ever.

A friend of mine said a show about life without a dad would just be the mom doing everything as usual only with less money and nobody to cut the grass.

We're all familiar with Man Bashing 101. They don't notice what needs doing around the house. They can't keep up with the master schedule. And they're hopelessly incompetent when it comes to emotional issues.

Women, on the other hand, are such a daily presence in family life even a moment's absence causes everything to unravel. Which might explain why I can't even go to the bathroom alone and my husband can sit on the couch and read the paper uninterrupted for hours.

But you have to wonder, if men don't have much of a role at home, maybe it's because we haven't given them the space to create one. How comfortable would you be taking over the helm of a ship from an experienced captain? Especially if you didn't know the starboard from the port and had only just recently learned to swim. Add to this the fact that the ship is constantly being hit by unpredictable storms, it's got a surly crew, and the captain is sore at you for your poor performance the last time you tried to drive. Even Gilligan wouldn't volunteer to take over that boat.

Shows and movies about a missing mom work because women are the chief processors of family emotions. They figure out how everybody feels and what we should do about it. When women aren't around, everything that was going on internally with everybody else now has to come out. The resulting tension and humor creates endless scenarios and plot lines.

But real family life isn't a sitcom, and everybody pays a heavy price when mom is the only one who knows how to deal with emotions. As women, it's hard not to immediately exercise our skills. As the entertainment industry and real life prove, our families would be lost without us.

While it may be touching to watch the TV dad step into the emotional realm, real life men deserve the same chance. And they shouldn't have to wait for the wife to keel over to take it.

20

Is Fake the New Real?

"Advertising may be described as
the science of arresting human intelligence
long enough to get money from it."

—STEPHEN LEACOCK

Pathological Botox Moms Wreak Havoc at PTA

Can Botox make you a better liar? The United States Armed
Forces says yes.

According to former US Army interrogation instructor Greg
Hartley, "The face involuntarily leaks emotions in easily iden-
tifiable patterns." So, while a down-turned mouth or wrinkled
brow would give away the average Joe or Jane, a Botox-injected
tennis mom may be able to get away with murder.

Unless, of course, you notice the French-manicured hands
clenched in her lap.

When people lie, their bodies and their mouths are out of
sync. Their brain is focusing so hard on creating the lie that
it can't control what the rest of their body is doing. So when
a normally animated person becomes still or a calm person
starts using herky-jerky gestures, chances are you've caught
them in a fib.

We all lie. It's part of what holds society together. Any man who's ever been asked, "Do these pants make me look fat?" knows that sometimes a good lie is the honorable thing to do. And if Aunt Marge goes to her grave thinking everybody loves her meatloaf, well, who's the wiser?

Little lies may smooth over tricky social situations, but bigger lies, like falsifying your resume or hiding money from your spouse, usually come back to haunt us. And whoppers like extramarital affairs and embezzlement carry such high risks, it's amazing that anyone even tries.

Hartley, author of *How to Spot a Liar*, suggests that, "People lie for three reasons—love, hate, or greed," and, "Self-preservation is a form of self-love that ranks at the top of the list."

When Joe from the mail room tells the crowd at the class reunion that he's about to make partner in his firm, he isn't necessarily pathologically possessed; he's just trying to save face with the former football players.

Self-preservation also explains why everyone on Cupid. com claims to be tall, talented, and toned. Hartley (GregHartley.com) suggests, "Internet dating takes our most primitive behavior—our sex drive—and puts it on the most modern platform." The result? Web sites filled with thin, blond, twenty-seven-year-old women and iron-pumping men with six-figure incomes.

While it may be challenging to weed out lies in dating profiles, it's a bit easier when you're face to face. Inexperienced liars trying to cover minor sins like staying out too late with the boys or pretending they really don't know who ate the last cookie dart their eyes, change their tone of voice, alter their rate of speech, and fidget when they fib.

But really good liars—like serial cheaters and car salesmen—typically only reveal their falsehoods in their face. And even then, you have to be quick to catch it. When a pro is caught in a lie, their faces go instantly blank, and their pupils dilate as they rearrange their mask.

It only lasts a second, but if the face of the guy you're about to sign a franchise deal with freezes when you ask about costs, get a lawyer to look over the contract before you sign.

As for the Botox-injected, country club moms, their permanently arched eyebrows might camouflage fabrications about family finances. But because children typically learn to read facial expressions from their mother, a woman who doesn't have any could be setting her offspring up for a lifetime of playing the patsy. Kids who've never seen a wrinkled forehead have a hard time interpreting what one means.

Passing off a lie may help you save face at PTA, but learning how to spot a fib is the real life lesson.

Television: Parallel Universe to La-La Land
And we're live in five, four, three, two, one...It's showtime! Ignore the crowd, the flashing red light on the camera, and the twenty million viewers, and pretend you and the host are best friends having an informal chat in her living room.

Welcome to the world of talk show television, the most bizarre out-of-body experience you can ever imagine. Being a faux celebrity isn't easy. Real celebrities either get used to the pressure, or they turn to drugs to numb the pain. But for faux celebrities like me, a guest spot on national TV leaves you feeling like you need a one-on-one with Dr. Phil. You wouldn't believe how much work it takes to appear natural.

I recently did a spot on a "big, national TV show." After a few appearances on local TV, I realized what works in real life doesn't translate well to TV. My spontaneous arm gestures that help me connect with a lecture audience come across as downright hysterical. And the furrowed brow I get while paying attention makes me look like I'm plotting to attack the host rather than trying to listen to her.

So this time, I engaged the services of a highly paid media coach to teach me how to camouflage my real self, so I would appear natural on TV.

I paid three hundred bucks an hour for her to coach me on how to laugh without opening my mouth so wide, how to avoid the bobble head and double chin syndrome by pretending I was wearing an invisible neck brace, and how to contain my hand gestures to a six-inch radius—all so I'll look more natural on camera.

You should also know that what appeared to be a casual back-and-forth chat with the host was the result of a script that went through five revisions and three production meetings. My catchy lines, although technically written by me, had been planned weeks in advance and were printed on huge cue cards being waved about by an underpaid production assistant. A teleprompter fed the host a stream of witty questions, also written by me and e-mailed weeks in advance.

And the moment in which I "spontaneously" threw my prop—a Barbie-style Queen of Perfect crown—into the studio audience was choreographed during a rehearsal where it took me five tries to learn how to throw a plastic crown in a way that captures the best camera angle.

Three coats of mascara and enough pancake makeup to fill an Aunt Jemima bottle kept me from looking like a corpse. Off camera I looked like an aging hooker, but on TV

I looked more or less like myself, although I swear the camera adds twenty pounds, not ten.

All this for a seven-minute segment about being your authentic self and connecting with real friends. When they introduced me as the author of *Forget Perfect*, the irony was not lost on me.

TV is the ultimate fake universe. But for some reason we continue to use it as a benchmark for real life. When people wax on about the '50s they usually refer to June Cleaver rather than their own mothers. *Little House on the Prairie* may have been a real book about a real family, but the show took a couple hundred people twelve hours a day to produce. Michael Landon was a nice guy, but he was also married three times. Even so-called reality shows take hours of editing to capture the most enticing clips.

Intellectually, we know this, but the TV beckons us as the ultimate happy place where problems are solved in thirty minutes and quick sound bites take the place of sage advice from our elders.

I hope my segment gave somebody out there something to think about and helped make their life a little bit better, and I'll continue to go on every show that will have me. But I also hope I never confuse la-la land with reality. It takes vats of makeup, hundreds of neurotic, overworked people, and a heavy dose of fantasy mixed in with gallons of coffee to create that surreal universe.

Your real life may not be as visually appealing as TV, but when you get old and overweight, you still get to keep your part. This life isn't some less-than-glamorous rehearsal—it's showtime.

21

Is Religion Stealing our Spirituality?

"There's no such thing as a soul.
It's just something they made up to scare kids,
like the boogeyman or Michael Jackson."

—BART SIMPSON

Social Neurosis Leads to Mass Destruction

Sigmund Freud called religion "a universal, obsessional ritual," saying, "Religion protects people from individual neurosis by being a kind of social neurosis."

Free thinkers often cast a cynical eye toward organized religion. With a legacy that includes holy wars, witch burnings, and other unsavory activities, it would be easy to say that religion, not money, is the root of all evil. Any intelligent person can tell you the darker side of organized religion isn't faith itself; it's the misguided, sometimes certifiably insane leaders who create the problems. It would be easy to say the fanatics are the bad guys, Mother Teresa is one of the good guys, and the problem isn't religion; it's some of the people running it. But people are a religion.

The word religion comes from the Latin root word *religare*, which means to tie together again, to bind back. And *Webster's* defines religion as "any specific system of belief, worship, or conduct, often involving a code of ethics or philosophy."

New religions typically start when a group of rabble-rousers perceives the church hierarchy as hopelessly out of touch. They decide to strike out on their own in search of a more meaningful connection with the divine. There's often a fight, sometimes people even get killed, and what emerges is a new faith with its own set of rituals and beliefs.

People start with very good intentions, but then two things take over: impatience and ego.

When people internalize a new set of beliefs that improves their lives, the better side of their human nature inspires them to share it with others. Whether it's a new diet, the teachings of the Bible, or the practice of meditation, whenever someone benefits from something new, they quite naturally want to spread the good word to others.

While it may have taken them months or even years to painstakingly incorporate the information into their own lives, once they know it, they often expect others to jump from the idea to the execution in two seconds flat. Most of us are impatient when it comes to waiting out the self-discovery processes of others.

Ego comes into play when people start to believe their primary role is to tell everybody else how they should be adhering to the agreed upon belief system, rather than leading by example and applying the principles to their own activities.

The purpose of religion is to provide people with a language, a process, and a community that supports them in deepening their spirituality. Religion is not inherently good or bad. It's a tool, much like a hammer. You can beat somebody over the head with it, or you can use it to build a house. Organized religion is at its best when it helps people move beyond their outer selves to discover their inherent spiritual beauty within. It's a tool that can help you unlock the secrets of the human soul and provide you with a closer connection to the divine.

When religion is presented as the ultimate answer instead of a tool, problems arise. People either cling to it fanatically or reject it outright. Impatience and ego on the part of some church leaders may have stolen our spirituality, but it was our own impatience and ego that let them take it.

How many of us have turned away from religion because it wasn't presented in a manner we found appealing? And how many times have we disregarded a universal truth simply because it came to us through a less-than-perfect teacher?

Are we even willing to try to employ the discipline of applying spiritual practices to our daily lives? Because discipline is what it takes to study, internalize, and live the principles of any given religion.

But that's when our ego steps in to help us out. Our ego serves as a handy cover for our lack of discipline. It's our ego that separates us from others. And it's our ego that tells us those rules are okay for other people, but "I've got enough brains to map out my own moral standards." Our ego doesn't want us to get beyond our outer self and open up our soul because that puts us in a vulnerable position.

It's hard to refute the historical or anecdotal evidence that when people embrace their innate spirituality, they lead happier and more productive lives. Whether or not we want to admit it, there's a soul inside each and every one of us. A soul with a very special purpose.

Religion can be a tool to help our souls shine. But are we willing to exert the discipline to patiently put aside our egos and let it?

Five Rules for Choosing a Bathing Suit or a Religion

Is it harder to choose a bathing suit or a religion?

I spent a Sunday afternoon comparing and contrasting the major brands of both, and I'm here to tell you, it's harder to find a bathing suit that fits you than it is a religious community.

In the time-honored, spring tradition of aging women, I spent several humiliating hours parading half-naked in front of three-way mirrors and fluorescent lights. I haven't bought a bathing suit in more than three years, so I was disappointed to learn that despite the much-heralded advances in tummy technology, none of the "control" panels could reduce the size of my abdomen by any more than the thickness of a single potato chip.

I also discovered that there's no place to put a floppy, middle-aged bosom in any of the cute suits. You can shove it to the sides, where it spills out under your armpits, making you look like you have a double bout of goiters. Or you can push it up and towards the front for the Anna Nicole Smith effect—only, in my case, the cleavage is ghostly white with blue veins, sort of like a cross between Anna Nicole and her late husband.

After giving up on flattering and settling for least offensive, I headed home only to discover that while bathing suit decisions have become harder and harder, choosing a religion is getting easier every day.

While I was in the dressing room struggling with three ounces of lycra, my thirteen-year-old daughter was on the couch comparison-shopping for a faith.

Thanks to Wheel O' Wisdom (KnockKnock.biz), judging the almighties is now as simple as a quick spin of a cardboard wheel.

The eight-inch, "Choose Your Religion" spinner consists of two printed cardstock wheels joined together in the center by a stainless steel grommet, allowing you to rotate the top wheel and view the perks, drawbacks, afterlife promises, and accessories for thirty of the major faiths. It also provides a brief description of each religion and shows you how many "potential new friends" you'll have if you sign up.

Thinking about Shintoism? You won't have to worry about attending regular services, but on the downside, there's "an ever present responsibility to uphold the ancestral honor."

Want to worship at the altar of Consumerism? You'll be disappointed to learn that "credit overuse begets spiritual bankruptcy," but the good news is, you have 912,868,813 new friends to join you at the church of debt.

The "Choose Your Religion" wheel refers to itself as a "Guide for the Savvy Convert," and it allows you to "base your religious choices on the things that really matter—what you'll wear, whether you can have sex, and where you go when you die."

My daughter and I were disappointed to learn that our faith, Unitarian Universalism, has fewer followers than Voodism. On the plus side, we've got better paraphernalia than the Snake Handlers. But my question is: If we can sound byte religion for the masses, why can't we make choosing a bathing suit just as simple?

I think we can. So, in the interest of spiritual development and being comfortable by the pool, here are my five guidelines for choosing a bathing suit—or a religion:

1. **COMPARISON SHOP.** What looked good on you as kid or what works for your neighbor isn't necessarily the best style for you.

2. **DON'T SETTLE FOR HAND-ME DOWNS.** Just because your mother picked it out for your sister twenty-five years ago doesn't mean you have to wear it.

3. **CHOOSE A BRAND WITH WOMEN ON THE DESIGN TEAM.** Products created solely by men often fail to provide the support a woman really needs.

4. **GO WITH YOUR GUT.** Even if your husband thinks it's a great fit, you don't have to take it home.

5. **LOOK FOR SUPPORT, NOT CONTROL.** Shifting yourself around a bit is okay, but if it contorts your innards into an uncomfortable position, it will only become more painful and binding with time.

Swaggart and Sororities: Too Tempting to Resist

What do Jimmy Swaggart, a beer-guzzling frat boy, and Hootie Johnson have in common?

They'll let you into their club—but don't invite any of "those people" to come along.

Just as Chip from Delta Tau Delta keeps the math geeks at bay, Hootie, the Augusta National Golf Club chair, keeps golfers safe from the likes of blacks and women. You can call it racist, sexist, bigoted, or elitist, but it doesn't matter whether it's coming from a religious leader, a guy with a green jacket, or a nineteen-year-old who just spilled Hunch Punch all over his khakis—telling your associates that membership in your club is proof of their superiority is one of the most effective recruiting techniques around.

In an *AARP* magazine article, author Karen Armstrong, a former nun-turned-religious scholar says, "There are some people, I suspect, who would feel obscurely cheated, if, when they finally arrived in heaven, they found everybody else there as well."

"Heaven would not be heaven unless those who reached it could peer over the celestial parapets and watch other unfortunates roasting below," obsersves Armstrong.

This thought process shows up everywhere from middle school cliques to world affairs. The better part of our nature wants to belong, but then once we get in, our evil twin takes over and tries to keep everybody else out. For some reason it's hard to feel good about ourselves, or our group, unless we think we've got one up on the rest of the world.

Imagine the Kappa Gammas telling a prospective pledge, "Yes, we are a fine group of young women, but we're actually no better than the Zetas or the Tri-Delts down the way. And for that matter, all the girls who didn't pledge a sorority are equally valued human beings as well."

We all want to feel special and to think that we've been chosen—whether it was by God or the rush chairman. We want to believe that somebody important looked out over the whole universe and picked us to be part of their club.

Yet as much as we may crave love and acceptance, a little part of us can't believe we deserve it just for being ourselves. We want to get in, but we think we've got to earn it, so we're willing to jump through all kinds of hoops to prove we're worthy.

Wearing a red lacy thong on your head for a week or

driving all the senior sisters to class every day seems like a small price to pay to be part of the cool crowd. And if you're looking for eternal bliss, it's only natural to assume the standards are even higher.

However, once a club or group gives us the coveted two thumbs up, we often feel the only way we can continue to keep it special is by keeping others out.

If they open the doors and let everybody else in, we'll be right back to square one—just another one of the bungling masses. Is our faith in ourselves and our fellow humans so limited that we require a group stamp of approval just to feel like we belong? And are our minds so small that we think being special is enhanced by limiting it to a small group of people?

It might be nice to believe that a religion, country club, or social group chose you because you're better than everybody else or that you chose them and earned your way in because you are a superior human being. However cute they may be, the Zeta Tau Alphas don't have a lock on partying and sisterhood anymore than one religion has exclusive rights to morality and spiritual truths. The truth is, most of our group affiliations—be they religious or social—reflect more about our economic status, geography, and upbringing than they do the core of who we really are.

It's tempting to buy into it when someone tells you that becoming one of them will make you special, particularly if you don't believe you already are.

Being part of a group can be a wonderful thing, whether it's people to worship with, a community to support you as you face life on your own, or folks who share your favorite hobby. But if the main motivation of an organization is to maintain its exclusivity, that rotten foundation eventually will eat away at the very feeling of camaraderie groups are meant to create.

Augusta National Golf Course finally did let some blacks in, and it looks like women may be next. I have no doubt the barriers we've erected to separate us are gradually coming down, but I have to wonder if our imagery of heaven as a gated community will ever go away.

As long as we're convinced that Saint Peter is sitting in a guard shack, checking off names before he lets people in, we're never going to be completely confident of our own ability to get through. But at a certain point, doing background checks and raising and lowering the gate becomes more trouble than it's worth. God has better things to do with Her time than protecting the exclusivity of Her community.

She's got some big news to share with Brother Swaggart and Pledge Class President Chip. Now, if only She could track down Hootie to set up a tee time, She could invite all Her pals up to the club to play.

Thou Shalt Not Think For Thy Self

Would you rather be told what to do or what not to do?

If you're like most of us, you probably don't respond well to criticism and negative reinforcement. Ask me to go dig a hole, and I might do it. But endlessly harping on me to quit being so lazy doesn't exactly inspire me to get off the couch.

It's a proven truth that people respond better to a positive vision of how they could be than to negative directives on how they shouldn't be. Good parents know they're better off nicely telling a two-year-old, "Color on the paper, Suzie," than screaming at her, "Keep those markers of my clean

wall!" And successful business leaders understand that barking at employees to "quit acting like no-talent losers" doesn't
have the same motivational effect as describing the potential
payoffs for great performance.

Despite obvious evidence of this universal human truth,
many religions have historically taken a "though shalt not"
approach to spirituality. It's easy to see why they might make
that mistake. After all, directives like, "Thou shalt not kill,"
and, "Thou shalt not steal," are pretty good advice no matter
what your faith.

But living your life in the land of "not" doesn't provide
people with a template for a positive contribution, much
less the motivation or inspiration to grow. As every good
teacher knows, if all you do is recite the rules every day,
your class won't learn a bloody thing. However, what would
happen if all religious leaders shifted from externally man-
dated commandments to teaching internally embraced
commitments?

In his book, *The Ten Commitments*, author David Simon
does exactly that. He takes each of the traditional Ten
Commandments and suggests a replacement "personal commitment." "Thou shalt not bear false witness against thy
neighbor," becomes, "I commit to truth." "Thou shalt not
commit adultery," translates into, "I commit to love."

The difference between a commandment and a commitment model is both subtle and staggering as the same time.
It's about externally driven rules versus an internalized spiritual model.

In the commandment mentality, as long as I don't take
the witness stand and tell lies about my fellow suburbanites,
I'm okay. But a commitment to truth requires a lot more

action on my part. I'm going to have to be just as truthful with my neighbors across the globe as I am with that annoying McKenzie family down the street. Additionally, anyone who's been married for any length of time will tell you that a true commitment to love is a lot more challenging than simply agreeing not to fool around.

Dr. Simon, medical director and co-founder of the Chopra Center for Well Being, suggests, "The 'thou shalt not' model doesn't get people to experience their own sacred nature."

Dr. Simon's Ten Commitment model (found on Chopra. com) is so elegantly simple and profoundly true, I'm surprised no one thought of it before now. But then again, entrusting the rabble to make their own decisions isn't exactly something religious leaders have been clamoring for.

It's tempting to want to enforce spiritual rules on others, but external mandates about what not to do don't ignite the human spirit any more than they can get a seven-year-old to quit fidgeting. And frankly, the people arguing to put the Ten Commandments on the courthouse wall don't look all that peaceful and happy to me.

In a "thou shalt not" environment, all the creative energy that might be naturally directed towards doing something fabulous has nowhere to go. So it manifests itself into an overzealous mission to make everybody else behave. Sooner or later, the natives always revolt, and we're seeing more signs of it every day. Humanity is getting tired of being treated like a child, and, fortunately, we're also growing weary of acting like one.

Commandments chiseled into stone may keep you out of hell, but commitments etched in your heart can create heaven on earth.

Cracking the Code on Literal Lunacy

Did he or didn't he?

Buried beneath all the controversy surrounding *The Da Vinci Code* is the big question people have been too polite to ask out loud: Did Jesus have sex? My question is, why do we even care? About that, or any of the other theories presented in *The Code*?

What if we discovered that Jesus actually had thousands of lovers? Would it in any way lessen the power of his message? And if someone is suggesting that churches haven't always accurately reported the contributions of women, is this really new information?

In case you've been living under a rock, one of the more controversial plotlines in *The Da Vinci Code* (the book and the movie) is that Mary Magdalene was Jesus' wife and that together they had a child. She was a powerful disciple, not a prostitute as previously reported. Their bloodline survives to this day, and we've all been duped by a huge church conspiracy to cover it up.

Sorry if I ruined it for you.

As the debates rage on about what's fact and what's fiction in *The Da Vinci Code*, I continue to be both annoyed and amused by the legions of people who prefer to endlessly argue over the literal meaning of the Bible rather than spending their time putting the principles into action.

I'd think if you were really a fan of Jesus, you'd be delighted at the thought that he may have reproduced. Yet many are angered at the mere suggestion that the Bible is anything less than one hundred percent accurate, and to imply that Jesus would do anything as disgustingly human as having "relations" with a woman is downright blasphemous.

But the fact of the matter is, we know the Bible was compiled by humans. The original texts were actually written by several authors, many over a time period of between two and four hundred years after Jesus' death. And the original languages included Greek, Hebrew, and Aramaic, none of which are known for being easily translated into modern prose.

Combine multiple translations with the proven premise that history is always written by the winners—and up until lately, the winners in the big church game were men—and it's not implausible to think that they might have left a few things out.

The Bible didn't exactly come down from heaven by fax. However, if you read the red writing in the Bible—quotations that religious scholars generally agree represent the actual words of Jesus himself—you'll find great spiritual truths that transcend time, religion, and creative editing.

I personally think all the debate about what Jesus did or didn't do kind of misses the point. To me, Jesus represents the human potential. To argue that he was just a man denies his divinity, and to say that he was solely divine ignores his humanity.

I often wonder if these two conflicting views of Jesus— man or Lord—are convenient ways of letting us all off the hook. If we believe he's our Lord and no one can ever be as perfect as Jesus, why should we even try? And if he was a mere mortal like the rest of us slobs, then perhaps there is no such thing as the divine.

But what if we embraced the idea that Jesus was both human and divine? It might mean that maybe we are, too. And we can no longer make any excuses for not acting like who we really are—manifestations of God on earth.

Kind of scary, isn't it?

Jesus symbolized the spark of divinity in all of us. We don't need to know the literal truths of his life to understand and execute the conceptual beauty of his message.

He lived love, and he was killed by fear. What else do we really need to know?

22

Why is TV More Interesting Than Church?

"God is a comedian playing to an audience too afraid to laugh."

—VOLTAIRE

From Phil to Phil: A Televised Look at Human Evolution

Is TV getting better or am I getting dumber?

After a ten-year hiatus from television, I'm back on the couch. And I'm fast renewing my love affair with my former flame: the boob tube. Who knew it contained such vital information? When last I left my flickering friend, I was disillusioned by the stupid jokes and overused laugh tracks. But now I have found personal enlightenment.

I've morphed from a wannabe intellectual, who disdainfully said she didn't have time for mindless TV, to a woman who considers *Queer Eye for the Straight Guy* a public service announcement.

Have I gotten lazier? You better believe it. But like an old boyfriend who matures into a surprisingly sophisticated man, the constant companion of my youth has undergone an extreme makeover as well.

Television always has reflected our social values. Actually, it reflects what a few rich, middle-aged white men think we value. But in the past, TV images were so powerful and appealing, many of us tried to model our lives after them. But as the little black box grew into a large, gray flat-screen, one-dimensional characters started making way for people who thought and acted a little more like us. And by the time the forty-eight inch plasma came barreling into our living rooms, it brought real people with it.

Now, the characters on TV don't just look like your neighbors, in some cases they actually are. You can talk all you want about how awful reality TV is, but there's an upside many us of aren't even aware of: It provides a mirror into our own lives. I'm not talking about *The Swan* or which skinny blonde chooses which hunky stockbroker to be her eternal love. Those shows are more manufactured than *Leave It to Beaver* ever was.

I'm talking about the television in which real people—with all their angst, talents, problems and creativity—try to get better, get ahead, or at the very least, get over whatever seems to be ailing them. Whether it's recovering stolen self-esteem on *Starting Over* or learning that everybody doesn't run their house the way you do on *Wife Swap*, seeing other people deal with their problems gives us a better understanding of our own. And for people who insist on constantly comparing themselves to the Joneses, reality TV can offer better benchmarks than Mike and Carol Brady.

Until I watched *Clean Sweep*, I thought I had the only family who couldn't use their dining room. And although

I'm still not changing my sponges as often as I should, the next time somebody asks me, *"How Clean is Your House?"* I can answer with confidence, "Not as filthy as that Cleveland couple with all the cats."

We humans are visual by nature. Seeing is believing, and sometimes it's the only way we can process new information. I've read fashion mags for years, but it took three rounds of middle-aged women being told *What Not to Wear* before I realized I shouldn't tuck my T-shirts into my jeans anymore. And if my fellow church board members knew how much the egomaniac *Apprentice*s helped me curb my control-freak tendencies, they'd probably send Donald Trump a personal thank you.

In both cases, I couldn't "get it" until I saw somebody exactly like me doing it wrong. The reality craze has done more than just provide the networks with cheap programming; it's brought the language of self-help to the general public. Topics that once were only fodder for shrink conferences are now part of our everyday vocabulary. And advice you used to pay for now comes into your home for free.

Our parents never knew they were co-dependent or dysfunctional, or even that they had "issues," because they didn't even have the words to describe it. They didn't get to watch thirty-seven video clips of the problem, with tips to solve it superimposed on the screen. If my mom had a *Nanny 911* hotline, I'm sure she would have dialed up a *Super Nanny* every day.

The TV self-improvement craze started when a guy named Phil put real people up on stage to talk about their problems and provided experts to help them through it. I'm not talking about Dr. Phil McGraw; I'm talking about Phil

Donahue, whose 1970s talk show was the precursor to what we see today.

Now, instead of having to discover our own solutions after a lifetime of problems, savvy producers edit twenty-five hours of mundane angst into three minutes of raw emotion. Set it to music, add graphics, and you're at the "aha" moment faster than ten years of therapy.

The circle of Phils—it's human improvement in progress.

TV is getting better. It's taught me how to discipline my kids, camouflage my tired eyes, and plan a theme wedding on just $5,000. I've acquired all the skills I need to improve my life. Now, if only I could put down the remote and start doing it.

Mobile Home Mea Culpa: Redneck Redemption

Confession is good for the soul. And it makes for pretty good TV, too.

The success of NBC's sitcom *My Name is Earl* demonstrates that the innate desire to confess your sins transcends all religious and cultural barriers. If you've been spending your evenings listening to the symphony or watching PBS, you might not be familiar with this TV phenom. But those of us in the beer-and-Cheetos crowd are parked on the couch every Thursday night to watch the karmic comedy of Earl Hickey as he navigates his way through his chicken-wing-and-trailer-park world trying to rectify his lengthy list of lifetime misdeeds.

Earl (played by Jason Lee) calls it karma. I call it Redneck Redemption. And I'm hoping that if a few members of my extended family are watching, the idea might catch on. There's something deeply satisfying in seeing someone come clean about their evil ways.

Whether it's your sister-in-law finally admitting that, yes, she intentionally tried to grab the limelight at your engagement party or your co-worker confessing that he stole your ideas for the Mr. Spuds account or even your kids revealing that they were the culprits behind "The Case of the Missing Count Chocula"—we like it when other people admit they did wrong. In fact, sometimes we like it so much we think it's our job to expose the true nature of their sins. It's like we have a divinely inspired need to seek the truth, but we'd rather point the finger out than in.

There's an honesty angel sitting on our one shoulder telling us to make things right in the world. But there's a "protect our ego at all costs" devil sitting on the other, saying, "Don't point the lie detector back at me."

Co-workers who cover up their mistakes drive us nuts. Spouses who refuse to acknowledge their character defects keep our stomachs in knots. And family members who rewrite the past and get away with it leave us fuming long after Thanksgiving dinner is over.

The lies and misdeeds of others are like a crusty scab we can't help but pick. We know we shouldn't scratch it, but we desperately want to yank it off and expose the ugly underbelly for all the world to see. Yet when it comes to ourselves, we often prefer to keep the band-aid on tight.

It's no coincidence that taking a fearless moral inventory and making amends is an integral part of all the twelve-step programs. Confess and repent is one of the great spiritual truths of all time.

Long before Jerry Springer got Bubba to admit he was the daddy and before Bill had to plead for mercy from Hil, Jesus said, "Know the truth, and the truth shall set you free."

While many of His followers have tried to beat the truth out of others in the name of their Lord, the operative word in His original directive was "you." Just like Earl Hickey, Jesus knew that the karma doesn't start flowing in the right direction until you come clean with yourself. I'm not sure what Jesus would say if he saw Earl towing a thirty-foot wiener down the highway with his drunk buddy straddled on top, as he did in one episode. But I'm pretty positive he would concur with the Buddhists and the Hindus, who believe that all living creatures are responsible for their own salvation.

Pointing the finger at others never provides the inner peace we humans crave. The only way you can achieve that is by cleansing your own soul.

But isn't that the way spiritual truths always work? You can share them with others, but their true power comes from applying them to yourself. So pass the Fritos, I've got three episodes of *Earl* on my TIVO, and I'm just aching to see if his trashy ex-wife finally gets what she deserves.

Is Televised Self-Help Taking the Place of Religion?

I think God is a large black woman, and She sent Oprah down to spread the love. The last guy She sent wasn't too media savvy, so this time God decided She would send us a sound byte specialist, a master marketer to help us shape up.

Truth be told, very few of us are living up to our true spiritual or emotional potential. In fact, most of us are wandering around so disconnected from our own souls, we've forgotten how wonderful we actually are.

When the Oprahs and the Dr. Phils of the world give us a new insight, they're simply tapping into the universal truths our spirit already knows. They create an emotional connection that helps us look at our lives with new clarity.

But is televised self-help taking the place of religion? It very likely might if churches can't stay true to the missions they were founded on. People turn to self-help, meditation, religion, and even drugs for the very same reason: We have a hole in our hearts, and we want some help in filling it.

New faiths and governments form when people become tired of the oppressive, restrictive forces of the current infrastructure and start rumbling for a change.

The serfs of Rome risked death following a long-haired, anti-establishment guy named Jesus, just as the colonists rebelled against the king of merry England to seek religious freedom in America.

Historically, nobody hangs around long when their group ceases to provide emotional connection. But have you ever seen someone who truly embraces their faith with all their heart? They shine. However, simply going through the motions of religion with just your head never creates that inner glow.

As human beings, we crave rituals and even rules. Meaningful ceremonies and established codes of conduct can free our minds from the mundane and help expand our understanding of the universe. And religion can provide us with a structure to deepen our personal connection with the divine.

Yet many of us turn away from organized religion. We find it boring, meaningless, and unenlightening. But is it religion that causes us to disconnect? Or is it the people running it?

We're drawn to leaders who accept us as we are, and who

give us the opportunity to grow into who we want to be. But we can't grow by blindly following rules created by someone else. We have to examine things with our own minds and make decisions based on our own inner compass before we can accept who put the compass there in the first place. Religions that start with the rules and offer no room for free will don't serve as vehicles for spiritual growth.

We know in our hearts that we were meant to live in love, not fear. And we have an inner longing to comprehend our role in the universe at large. True messengers of God understand the fine art of providing group spiritual direction while at the same time encouraging personal self-discovery. Whether in the pulpit or on TV, they come to us in the time and places we need them most. Their words and deeds may not be perfect, but their wisdom prompts us to question the status quo. They help us move beyond the crazy restrictive ideas we humans get into our heads by tapping into the emotions lying dormant in our souls.

God wants nothing more for us than what we secretly desire for ourselves—a life of meaning and love. So She sent down one of her best girlfriends to support the effort.

23

Is God a Small, Sassy Black Woman?

"While I know myself as a creation of God,
I am also obligated to realize and remember
that everyone else and everything else
are also God's creation."

—MAYA ANGELOU

Hero Factory Staffed with Stand-Up Citizens

Housekeeper to hero. Domestic to dignitary. Rosa Parks was many things in her life, but she wasn't tired.

The romanticized version of her story is that when Parks refused to give up her seat on that Alabama bus, it was a single act of defiance by a poor-but-proud seamstress too exhausted from her hard day's work to get up and move to the "colored" section in the back. But the real story is that Rosa Park's bold actions on December 1, 1955, and the yearlong bus boycott that ensued were part of a carefully orchestrated plan that was years in the making. Community leaders had been planning a bus boycott, and they were waiting for just the right person to give the movement momentum.

Enter Parks, a well-respected woman with a spotless record, who was a former secretary of the Montgomery chapter of the NAACP.

It's not certain whether Rosa Parks' refusal to give up her seat on the bus was planned for that day or whether years of civil rights work spontaneously burst forth in a shining movement of bravery. What is certain is that the people in Parks' community created an environment that allowed her to come forward, and their well-organized actions immediately following her arrest leveraged her courageous stand.

As human beings, we all want to believe one person can make a difference, and Rosa Parks certainly did. Her actions that day in Montgomery helped unleash the power of the civil rights movement. But did Rosa launch the movement? Or did the movement launch Rosa?

The truth is, the hero doesn't create the environment; the environment creates the hero. And believe it or not, the prospects for future heroes are actually looking pretty good these days.

My daughter's first-grade class was studying the civil rights movement, and I happened to be volunteering one day when they were discussing Martin Luther King Jr. As I sat in the back stapling construction paper birds to a huge poster of blue sky, her teacher read a story about King as a young boy, told from the vantage point of his sister.

As the teacher described King's pain when the white boys he had befriended told him their dad had forbidden them to play with him anymore, the class was stunned. When the teacher went on to explain that blacks and whites used to go to separate schools, the kids were just amazed.

"How weird," they chimed. "Why would you divide people up like that?"

As they pondered the absurdity of this bizarre system they held out their arms, side by side, trying to decide who would go to the white school and who would go to the black one. Their little spindly six-year-old arms varied in color from dark brown to pale alabaster.

Would the girl from the Philippines with yellowish skin go to the white school or the black one? What about the boy from Mexico, whose skin was light tan? And then there was the black child with the white mother. If she went to the black school, would they let her mother in to pick her up?

It never even dawned on them that one school might be perceived as "better" than the other. When the teacher told them there was a time when blacks couldn't vote, the kids wondered, "Did they have their own president?"

As I looked at my little blue-eyed, blond daughter standing there with her class, unable to even fathom these incomprehensible social barriers, I realized just how far we had come. Her father, my husband, was raised in the Deep South. Born just one year before Rosa refused to move to the back of the bus, he went to segregated schools, his family had black maids who got a new uniform for Christmas, and whenever the yard help came to the back door for a drink, everyone knew you gave them a Mason jar because heaven forbid black lips touch a glass that your white family might drink from.

Yet one generation later his child sits next to a boy from Nigeria, befuddled by the idea that anyone would view them as anything but a pair of six-year-olds who like to draw.

Was my husband a rabble-rouser who fought against

the indignities of his childhood? No. He simply grew up. And as the world changed, so did he. Margaret Mead said, "Never doubt that a small group of thoughtful, committed citizens can change the world; indeed, it's the only thing that ever does."

The heroes of tomorrow are being created in the environment of today. And you don't have to be a Rosa Parks to do your part. All you have to do is decide that you're not too tired to take a stand.

Presidential Bonnet Opens the Door for Generations of Queens

She was wearing a lime green and aqua blue, paisley, polyester dress and panty hose with the reinforced toe sticking out of her white sandals. It was 1972, and her biggest problem wasn't the color of her shoes after Labor Day, it was the color of her skin all year long. That, and the fact that presidential candidates don't wear heels.

When Shirley Chisholm announced she was running for president back then, the most common reaction was, "President of what?" And when Walter Cronkite let the world know that America's first black congresswoman had her sights set on an even higher office, he actually said on the national news—and I swear I am not making this up—"A new hat, or rather a bonnet, was tossed into the presidential race today."

Most people my age don't even know who Shirley Chisholm is. Quite honestly, the main thing I remember about her campaign was my third-grade teacher telling us how historical it was. In hindsight, it took guts for her even to bring it up with a bunch of lily-white kids living in the suburbs. But my teacher was black, and for a woman who taught in an almost all-white school, Shirley Chisholm must have represented a miracle.

I don't exactly remember what she said—her comments fell into the Charlie Brown-style "WHA-WHA-WHA" teacher talk I usually chose to ignore. But I do remember the look on her face was very different than when she was talking about grammar.

I recently saw the film about the Chisholm campaign, *Chisholm '72: Unbought & Unbossed*, and as I watched the documentary, I was moved to tears, realizing for the first time how this determined, rather prim woman changed things forever.

"I ran because somebody had to do it first," Chisholm said.

One of my favorite clips in the movie is Chisholm describing a white congressman's reaction to her 1968 election to the House of Representatives.

"Mrs. Chisholm," he said, "Can you believe they pay you the same $45,000 they pay me?" Did he think she marched up the steps of the House so she could clean it?

I love her reaction: "Mr. Congressman," she retorted, "Yes, they are paying me the same 45 they're paying you, and I'm paving the way for more people who look like me to do the same thing."

Cut to forty years later, when Oprah Winfrey makes billions and has more power than the President of the United States. Lest you think I'm joking, consider what would happen if George Bush said we should all read a particular book. Half of America would roll their eyes and look the other way. But if Oprah says we need to pay attention, we're all ears.

Oprah may be the Queen of Talk, but Shirley Chisholm is one of the people who put her on the throne—something I'm sure Oprah is fully aware of and incredibly grateful for. Shirley Chisholm didn't just open doors for black women; she opened doors for all women.

Let's be honest here. Once white women saw a black woman make a serious run for the presidency, it wasn't too big a leap for them to realize they could do anything too. I'm humbled and amazed when I think about what she went through to blaze the trail for the rest of us.

Shirley Chisholm didn't win the 1972 Democratic nomination, but she did get enough delegates to speak at the National Convention in Miami—something no woman of color had ever done before.

George McGovern ended up with the party nomination and Richard Nixon won the presidency. Proof that just because your skin matches the paint on the building doesn't mean you deserve the Oval Office.

But the small woman in the white sandals put an idea into our consciousness: the idea that power doesn't always come in a gray suit. And that other people don't get to pick your destiny; it's something you choose for yourself.

Shirley Chisholm died Jan. 1, 2006. The movie about her life was completed just before she passed away. But the story she started has only just begun.

Is Living Paycheck to Paycheck a Crime Punishable by Death in Flood Water?

"It's their own fault, really. Why didn't those people just evacuate when they had the chance?" I overheard one woman saying to another in the line at the grocery store. I shielded my face with a box of frozen waffles and pretended to read the National Enquirer while I eavesdropped some more.

It was twenty-four hours after hurricane Katrina, and she, like many, was convinced that what we were seeing on the six o'clock news was merely Darwinism in action. The unfit were not surviving. Unfit people, like single mom Mable Brown.

Mable wanted to leave but couldn't get gas for her aging car; all the stations were closed. A New Orleans newcomer who had just moved there from Atlanta, Mable's instincts told her to take the twenty dollars she had in cash and get out. But her sisters had lived in New Orleans for years. They told her hurricanes were scary, but if they had candles, they would be okay.

But then the water started rising. Mable checked every twenty minutes and counted how many of the outside steps were covered up. When the water was up to the 7th step, she knew they were in trouble. But it was dark, and they couldn't leave their apartment and walk through the water in the pitch-black city.

"We knew there were alligators and snakes in the water because we were next to the bayou, so we were afraid to get in the water in the dark. We couldn't have seen where we were going."

So she and her sister went onto the porch and started fires with their furniture trying to flag down helicopters to rescue them and their six kids.

The next morning the water was up to step fourteen, Mable told the kids "Get up, put on long sleeve pants and shirts, put on some shoes, and we're going to walk through the water." At 5'6" the water was up to Mable's chin. Her two daughters, ages 8 and 13, could swim, so she dragged them along beside her.

Her sister and her niece couldn't swim, and they were too short to keep their heads above, so Mable got her sister's two older boys to put them on their backs. In water up to their necks, Mable told the group to feel for the sidewalk with their feet so they could keep their footing.

After they walked through the muck for an hour, they got to a dry bridge overlooking the Superdome. They waited for five hours, watching bodies float by, trying desperately to get one of the police cars or buses to take them out of the city. "We saw the buses, but they wouldn't let people on. One guy opened his door, and we thought we were going to get on, but they went to take all the prisoners out of the jails."

She decided to leave on her own, "I'm seeing bodies tied to the pole, so I said, 'If I have to walk all the way to Baton Rouge that was my plan.'" But then the water started rising on the other side of the bridge.

Mable asked policeman after policeman what to do, "but everybody told us something different. I kept seeing buses going toward the Superdome, so I realized that was where I better go."

As the crowd around them on the bridge got wilder and wilder, Mable gave up her spot on dry concrete, grabbed her sister, the six kids, and waded back down into knee high muck to get inside the dome with the hope that one of the buses would get her family to safety. Mable and the crew entered the dome and found utter mayhem. With buses sitting right outside, the crowd grew crazier by the minute. Everyone was panicking that the other levee near the dome was going to break and they would all be washed away. Bedlam broke out; guns were being fired inside the dome; there were no lights in the rest room.

"People were losing their kids. Crazy men were snatching kids, bringing them in the bathroom and raping them." A woman told Mable a two-year-old had died from rape. Mable kept her two daughters beside her.

"We were stuck together like glue."

Finally, they were told that the buses, still sitting right outside, would be loading in the morning. Sitting in a chair normally reserved for a screaming Saints fan, Mable spent the night with her arms wrapped around her two kids wondering if the levee was going to break, if the dome was going to catch fire, or worse, if she might fall asleep and lose her grip on her girls.

At four o'clock the next afternoon, after twenty-four hours in hell, Mable and her daughters were loaded like cattle on buses headed for Houston. Seven hours later Mable's bus pulled into the Astrodome parking lot. She was told to stay on the bus and wait until they could check her in.

"But I counted the number of buses and realized it would take forever for them to get to us, so I got my kids off, and we walked into the dome."

Mable checked herself in. They were provided showers, clothes, and food. "They were out of blankets, so they gave us sweaters. We found boxes, broke them apart, and laid the kids down." Mable managed to find her mother, and her other three sisters with their kids. All had made it onto buses to escape the Superdome.

Finally, at 3 a.m. that night, the whole family stretched out in a walkway and went to sleep. Mable woke up at dawn. They had volunteers helping them, but aside from food and water, there didn't seem much anyone could do.

That's when Mable decided she needed to figure a way

out. "I remembered seeing a Sprint store near the dome as buses came in." Mable had a Sprint phone somewhere lost in the muck of New Orleans. "I left my kids with my sister and walked two blocks over there and bought a new phone. They said they would charge my account $55.00."

"Once I got back, me and my sister started getting numbers off the bulletin board and calling."

She made some calls, tracked down the manager of the hotel she used to work for in Atlanta and got herself a job. Now, she just had to get there.

Mable called the South West Unitarian church office. She left a message on their machine saying that she wanted to get back to Georgia. They picked up the message that morning, and because they knew my suburban Atlanta congregation was trying to help people, they called me.

Forty-eight hours later with her girls tucked safely into my daughters' rooms, and her three sisters, her mother, and her twelve nieces and nephews sleeping in houses up and down my block, Mable Brown collapsed on my guest room bed.

I wish I could say I swooped in like a white knight and saved Mable, but I didn't. All I could do was use my Internet connection and my phone to run interference for the most resourceful woman in America as she saved herself—and eighteen members of her family.

While she and her family were still in Houston, I listened on the other end of her cell as she unsuccessfully tried to get a FEMA person to help her get on a bus to Atlanta, despite Mable telling her that Greyhound had specifically told us to check in with FEMA before booking and giving the woman the exact departure time of the Atlanta bus leaving the Greyhound station two miles away.

I waited while she asked the rest of her extended family if they wanted to take the word of a stranger on the phone and go to Atlanta where people they had never met were supposed to be waiting to take them into their homes.

After we gave up on FEMA and I bought the tickets myself, I talked to a desperate Red Cross worker who called everyone she could, but was finally forced to tell me they had no way to get Mable's family from the Astrodome to the Greyhound station.

I waited while the Houston Unitarian minister I found via Internet drove down to the Astrodome to search for Mabel and her family. I listened as he heartbreakingly told them that despite twenty phone calls to churches all over Houston, he couldn't corral a church bus to take nineteen of them to the Greyhound station in time to make the Atlanta bus. So after eight days of struggling, they now had to get themselves organized to take the light rail across the street from the dome to the bus station.

I agonized as the woman at the bus station ticket counter told Mable that because all the tickets had been paid for over the phone via credit card, she couldn't hold tickets for the sister whose family hadn't gotten there yet—even though the tickets had open-ended dates. I started to cry when I heard Mable breaking down, because the woman refused to talk to me.

I about fell out of my chair when I heard Mabel sniff away her tears and ask to speak to a supervisor. Telling her politely but firmly "I need you to put my sister's name on these tickets and hold them because I've got to get my kids on this bus."

I nervously sat by the phone for hours wondering if Mable had made it on the bus. I finally heaved a sigh of relief when Mable called from another number saying her phone had been cut off but she was on the bus and had borrowed a phone from a guy in the back row.

I seethed as I waited in line at the Sprint store.

I just about committed bodily harm when I discovered that Mable's phone had been cut off because all her minutes on the phone with me had put her over her prepaid account limit. The phone she had bought only one day earlier outside the Astrodome, while wearing her hurricane refugee bracelet and explaining to the clerk that her other phone had been lost in the muck when she swam her kids out of New Orleans.

I scrambled to get together our cooler of food when Mable called to tell me that because the bus didn't make any of the usual Louisiana stops, they were getting in three hours early. I wept when my minivan-driving, PTA friend and I finally wrapped our arms around Mable and her children.

I groaned when, coming out of the bus station—two white women who hadn't been in a bus station in fifteen years—I discovered the wheels on our vans were booted, because the guy who came up and told me to give him five dollars must not have been a parking attendant after all. I rolled my eyes when the real parking guy, who was watching the lot from across the street and must have booted our cars the second we went in the station, wouldn't take pity on two clueless suburban moms and a crowd of hurricane-shocked kids clinging to their mothers.

By the time I had written up Mable's story, my church had fed her family and all her sisters' families breakfast, and my neighbors had delivered nineteen duffel bags filled with clothes, toys, and toiletries And by the time her tale hit the newspapers and the Net, Mable had been asleep for sixteen hours straight.

I ended up with a $1400 Amex bill for the nineteen Greyhound tickets from Houston to Atlanta. I paid Sprint fifty bucks for putting Mable's phone back on, and my friend and I both grimaced when the ABS parking charge showed up on our Mastercards.

But if you'd have told me two weeks before Hurricane Katrina struck that $1500 and a phone call from a single mom who worked as a maid in New Orleans would transform my neighborhood and church into the kind of people we've always wanted to be, I would have written you a check on the spot.

And if you'd have told me that the bravest, smartest women I ever met was going to pay me a visit, I would have bought better sheets.

That first night, before they all went to bed, Mable's eight-year-old daughter asked me if the President was the one who finally got them out. I told her the truth, "Honey, the President didn't get you out, the Governor didn't get you out, the Mayor didn't get you out. Your mamma got you out of there."

∽

God is calling us to become the people we are capable of being.

Grace isn't something you find outside of you. You've had it since the day you were born; it's the shining life of your soul just waiting to be revealed.

May we find the grace to ignite the spark of divinity that resides within each and every one of us.

And may we never let our own dirty laundry stand in our way.

Recommended Resources

Cool people, books and websites that can make your life better without boring you or killing you in the process.

BrainTricks.com
David L. Weiner – Author, psychology writer, explainer of nutty human behavior

What drives so many apparently normal, intelligent people to act nuts? The boss who snorts around like a chimp or the nice PTA mom who shrieks at her kids every night. Whether it's you or someone you know, Wiener's work demonstrates why our biology often overrides our brains and what you can do about it.

Battling the Inner Dummy: The Craziness of Apparently Normal People
Reality Check: What Your Mind Knows but Isn't Telling You
Power Freaks: Dealing With Them in the Workplace or Any Place

BucketBook.com
Tom Rath – Author, Pollster, Positive Pal Pontificator

Using a simple model of a bucket and a dipper, Rath shows you how to be a better parent, a better boss, and a happier person. His Bucket book —a NY Times best seller—reveals how even the briefest interactions affect your relationships, productivity, health, and longevity, and *Vital Friends* demonstrates that water cooler time is more critical to your success than you might think.

How Full Is Your Bucket: Positive Strategies for Work and Life
Vital Friends: The People You Can't Afford to Live Without

Chopra.com
Dr. David Simon – Author, Choprah Center Medical Director, East meets West sage

Dr. Simon co-founder with Deepak Chopra of The Chopra Center provides a powerful positive take on the Ten Commandments. Instead of "thou shalt not" (eat too much, work too hard, etc.), Dr. Simon shows you how to change your mindset from commandments to personal commitments and make the personal transformations you always wanted.

The 10 Commitments: Translating Good Intentions into Good Choices

DeakGroup.com
Dr. JoAnn Deak – Author, educator, grower of great girls

Dr. Deak is renowned for her knowledge of what makes girls ages six to sixteen tick. Her book is a must-read for every parent raising a daughter, as she says, "Every interaction a child has, during the course of a day, influences the adult that child will become."

Girls Will Be Girls: Raising Confident and Courageous Daughters

DrNorthrup.com
Christiane Northrup, M.D. – Author, women's health expert, love-map-reading OB/GYN

An innovative leader in women's health. Dr. Northrup pioneered the partnership between conventional and complimentary medicine. Her website, newsletter, and best-selling books are quite simply the best information I've ever read to help you improve your physical and emotional health.

*Women's Bodies: Women's Wisdom, Creating Physical and Emotional Healing
Mother-Daughter Wisdom: Creating a Legacy of Physical and Emotional
Health*

FengShuiPalace.com
Karen Rauch Carter – Author, Feng Shui consultant, creator of "better luck"

Can tin foil under your couch save your marriage? Can planting a penny in your yard make you wise and rich? Karen Rausch Carter shows you how to put the right stuff in the right place to make your life sing. It's woo-woo, but it works!

*Move Your Stuff Change Your Life: How To Use Feng Shui To Get Love,
Money, Respect and Happiness*

Freakonomics.com
Steven Levitt – Economist, author, brainiest guy in America
Stephen Dubner – Author, writer, creative genius

From what makes a perfect parent and why do crack dealers live with their mothers? The snappy writing and fascinating research found in *Freakonomics* answer these questions and more. Steal a few lines off the *Freakonomics* blog, and you'll feel like the smartest person in the room the next time you go to a cocktail party.

Freakonomics, A Rogue Economist Explores the Underside of Everything

GettingTheLoveYouWant.com
Harville Hendrix & Helen LaKelly Hunt – Authors, counselors, savers of marriages

Oprah Winfrey included Hendrix's "Imago Theory" in her list of "Unforgettable! Oprah's Top 20 Shows" because it is literally a new way to love. Don't go to another boring finger-pointing marriage counselor again. Whether your marriage is happy or miserable, Imago can help you and your partner find the love and joy you deserve. Read the book, get the audio, buy the DVD and if you can, attend a weekend workshop, it will transform your marriage and your life forever.

Getting the Love You Want (book and workshop)
Through Conflict to Connection (DVD)

GregHartley.com
Greg Hartley – Author, interrogation expert, lie-catcher

Ever caught a spouse, business partner, parent, boss, or child lying right to your face? Hartley is a decorated military interrogator who now works as a business consultant. His book and seminars teach you how to tell if someone is lying, just by listening to them, and observing their actions and behavior (which is, sadly, a much-needed skill.)

How to Spot a Liar: Why People Don't Tell the Truth…and How You Can Catch Them

JohnSelby.com
John Selby – Author, teacher, meditative master to the masses

Selby combines meditative practices with business and personal wisdom to help you break through the barriers in your own mind. A spiritual teacher who understands that God comes to us with many names, Selby's on-line courses, lectures, seminars and books have been used by corporations and individuals. He is the author of over 30 books including:

Jesus for the Rest of Us (my personal favorite)
Take Charge of Your Mind
Quiet Your Mind
Seven Master One Path: Meditation Secrets from the World's Greatest Teachers

Judith Wallerstein – Author, researcher, truth-teller about divorce

If you're thinking of getting divorced, if you are divorced or if you were raised by divorced parents you owe it to yourself to read Wallerstein's book. It reads like a compelling novel, but her objective assessment about the impact of divorce on kids will forever alter your perceptions of the big D.

The Unexpected Legacy of Divorce: A 25 year Landmark Study
What About the Kids?: Raising Your Children Before, During, and After Divorce

LisaDaily.com
Lisa Daily – Dating Expert, wordsmith, author, love doctor with jokes

If you want to become one of those women men go ga-ga over, check out Lisa's site and find out how you too can become a Dreamgirl, no matter what your age. Forget the manipulative snag-a-man-at-any-costs relationship experts, Lisa is hilariously funny and offers real-world advice on how to improve your own life and attract a great guy at the same time.

Stop Getting Dumped: All You Need to Know to Make Men Fall Madly In Love and Marry the One In Three Years or Less.

LunchLessons.org
Chef Ann Cooper – Nutritionist, author, lunch lady on a mission

Chef Ann offers tips and techniques to get your kids, and your kids' school off the high fat, high starch, processed food routine. Committed to "changing the way we feed our children," Chef Ann's site provides menus and recipes that can take your family from deep fried Frankenfood to real food faster than you can say snap peas.

Lunch Lessons: Changing the Way We Feed Our Children
In Mother's Kitchen: Celebrated Women Chef's Share Beloved Family Recipes

MichaelAlvear.com

Michael Alvear – Columnist, author, TV personality, reviver of flat-line libidos

The co-host of the HBO's *Sex Inspectors,* Michael combines hilarious wit with practical advice to not only help you have more sex, but also make you *want* to have more sex. Warm enough to be a TV Sexpert, thoughtful enough to be an NPR commentator, and humorous enough to write a nationally syndicated column, Michael tells it like it is, and helps you make it happen the way you want it to.

Sex Inspectors Master Class: How to Have an Amazing Sex Life
Men Are Pigs But We Love Bacon

Paul-Coleman.com

Dr. Paul Coleman – Author, psychologist, intimacy expert for idiots

A well-known expert in intimacy and relationships, Dr. Coleman can help even an idiot achieve relationship success. He breaks it down into simple terms and helps you understand your own self-imposed obstacles to intimacy.

The Complete Idiots Guide to Intimacy

PersonalityType.com

Barbara Barron-Tieger & Paul Tieger – Authors, seminar leaders, Speed-readers of people

Ever wondered why your child acts the way they do, or why you hate a job everybody else says you should love? Personality Type is a (a) powerful tool that will make you happier and more successful in every aspect of your life, your career, your family, your children, your relationships. Knowing your "type" unlocks powerful insights that help you understand yourself and others as never before. The Tiegers books are literally life-changing:

Do What You Are: Discover the Perfect Career for You Through the Secrets of Personality Type
Just your type: Create the Relationship You Always Wanted Using the Secrets of Personality type
Nurture by Nature: How to Raise Happy Healthy Children Using the Insights of Personality Type

PRSecrets.com
Susan Harrow – PR guru, author, media coach to the stars

If you want to sell yourself without selling your soul, you need Susan Harrow. Her free 60 Second Secrets E-Zine is chock full of tips, and her E-books, audio tapes and tele-seminars give you the inside scoop on what it takes to get media attention without being a no-morals huckster. My favorites:

Sell Yourself Without Selling Your Soul (Hardcover)
Get a Six-Figure Book Advance (E-book)
The Ultimate Guide to Getting Booked on Oprah (Hard Copy and E-book)
Get into O Magazine (E-Book)

SusanReinhardt.com
Susan Reinhardt – Columnist, Author, Southern Belle Prone to Trash Talk

Susan is one of the funniest southern writers you'll ever read. A syndicated columnist with Gannett, her writing takes you on a wild ride through the trenches of motherhood, marriage, fading beauty, and even a nip and tuck or two.

Not Tonight Honey, Wait 'Til I'm a Size 6
Don't Sleep With a Bubba Unless Your Eggs Are in Wheelchairs

ThePeaceAlliance.org
Making peace sexy and saving the world from global annihilation

The campaign to create a United States Department of Peace is gaining momentum every single day. It's not a pipe dream, it's a bill in front of Congress, and in all likelihood will be a major issue in the 2008 Presidential race.

4-WomenOnly.com
Shaunti Feldhan – Author, columnist, tour guide to the male mind

Shaunti's book and in-depth surveys reveal shocking insights about what goes on inside the minds of men. If you ever wondered what's going on inside your man's head, read her material, you'll be amazed.

For Women Only: What You Need To Know About the Inner Lives of Men

Acknowledgements

There's a trend toward not including author acknowledgements in books anymore. I doubt it's because authors are ungrateful. Most of us are very much aware that books are never the work of just one person.

It's probably because when you start thanking a million people, you sound a bit like you're accepting an Academy Award, and most readers are bored to tears reading about how much you appreciate your family and friends.

But I've come to realize that acknowledgements aren't for the masses of readers; they're for those special few who helped you along the way. And although a book isn't as big an undertaking as a movie, it still means a lot to the people involved.

So at the risk of coming across like a pompous fool or even worse, forgetting someone, I decided I couldn't send this book to press without expressing my heartfelt thanks to the many people who have so generously blessed me with their time and talents:

The team at Jefferson Press, David Magee, Charlotte Lindeman, and Henry Oehmig, who not only helped shaped the concept and book, but also proved that Lookout Mountain can give New York City a run for the money any day of the week.

The Wasabi PR Team led by Drew Gerber and Michelle Tennant, storytellers to the media and marketers extraordinaire, whose keen insight shaped the brand and helped me get over myself and remember the core message.

Acro Media, whose fabulous web design upped my cool quotient exponentially.

Cover artist Joan Perrin-Falquet, who provided yet another beautiful interpretation of woo-woo meets wisecracking.

Kelly Poelker, VA to the stars, who made my life easier and took care of the details, so I could carve out time to write.

Jessica Carter, who by asking me to write a column, set the wheels in motion. I'll forever appreciate the opportunity you gave me.

Gwinnett Daily Post editors past and current, Kristen Roby, Rachel Mason, and Shelley Mann, who literally clean up my act every week, and publisher J. K. Murphy, who got me into the rest of the chain.

Buffalo News editor Liz Kahn, who picked up my column before anyone else and whose feedback on my writing pointed me toward wider syndication.

Fred Love, a dear friend with a million stories who came up with the idea for the book in the first place. I sure got my money's worth out of that dinner party.

Molly Schreck, the original cool chick and the best manager I ever had, whose support and uncanny understanding of human angst helped shape the early columns.

Susan Harrow, a PR goddess who taught me "the way it really works" and remains one of the most generous girlfriends I know.

Kate Snow, who is not only razor smart but also way funnier than middle America may ever know. Thanks for working around the rules and providing an endorsement. I'm glad we both made time to violate the "I'm not taking on any new friends" policy.

Michael Alvear, a loving and supportive friend whose wicked wit always inspires. How a TV star and gay "Sexpert" can keep a married middle-aged mommy grounded remains a mystery, but you do.

Betsy Bombeck, whose comment that day in Phoenix validated a lifetime of aspiration and whose on-going friendship has been a treasure.

My sister, Leslie Freymann, and my brother, Jim Earle, whose childhood antics inform much of my writing and whose adult friendships help keep me sane.

My parents, Jay and Judy Earle, whose unconditional support of my children, my husband, and me are models of what fabulous parenting and grandparenting are all about.

My two darling daughters, Alex and Elizabeth, who gracefully accept a frazzled mother with her head in the computer and her ear glued to a cellphone, and who provide gentle and not-so-gentle reminders to live what I write about.

My husband, Bob, whose keen insights about male behavior, unfailing BS detector, and meticulous proofreading made many of these essays much better. You truly are the love of my life, and I thank God every day for you and the team of skilled counselors who helped me appreciate you.

And the single most important contributor to this book, my dear friend, Lisa Daily. The most fabulous and funny writer I know, who graciously allows me to steal her best lines and who tirelessly contributes to "our column" week after week.

It's an honor to share a brain with you. I only wish that my half was as brilliant and creative as yours.